DATE DUE

PRE ⎢_____⎢_____⎢_____⎢_____⎢ FOR

PREPARING EDUCATORS FOR ONLINE LEARNING

A Careful Look at the Components and How to Assess Their Value

Edited by
Stacy Hendricks
Scott Bailey

ROWMAN & LITTLEFIELD
Lanham • Boulder • New York • London

Published by Rowman & Littlefield
A wholly owned subsidiary of The Rowman & Littlefield Publishing Group, Inc.
4501 Forbes Boulevard, Suite 200, Lanham, Maryland 20706
www.rowman.com

Unit A, Whitacre Mews, 26-34 Stannary Street, London SE11 4AB

British Library Cataloguing in Publication Information Available

Library of Congress Cataloging-in-Publication Data

Names: Hendricks, Stacy, 1970– editor of compilation.
Title: Preparing educators for online learning : a careful look at the components and how to assess their value / edited by Stacy Hendricks, Scott Bailey.
Description: Lanham : Rowman & Littlefield, [2016] | Includes bibliographical references.
Identifiers: LCCN 2015040432 (print) | LCCN 2015047220 (ebook) | ISBN 9781475822496 (cloth : alk. paper) | ISBN 9781475822502 (pbk. : alk. paper) | ISBN 9781475822519 (electronic)
Subjects: LCSH: Teachers–Training of–Computer-assisted instruction. | Teachers–Training of–Evaluation. | Teachers–Selection and appointment.
Classification: LCC LB1707 .P728 2016 (print) | LCC LB1707 (ebook) | DDC 370.71/1–dc23 LC record available at http://lccn.loc.gov/2015040432

♾ ™ The paper used in this publication meets the minimum requirements of American National Standard for Information Sciences Permanence of Paper for Printed Library Materials, ANSI/NISO Z39.48-1992.

Printed in the United States of America

CONTENTS

PREFACE

Many have said that a U.S. president's legacy is often best determined by the Supreme Court justices he (and someday she) appoints, since these justices remain active long after the president's tenure. Likewise, the most valuable contribution a school administrator makes to his or her school may well be grounded in the vacancies filled during that tenure. Whether it's a superintendent hiring principals or a principal hiring teachers, hiring well is critical to both the current and ongoing success of a school.

Given the paramount importance of hiring, school administrators seek to hire the most qualified candidates for both teaching and administrative positions. While many factors may huddle loosely under the umbrella of "most qualified," one of the primary considerations is the candidate's academic and technical training. Is the candidate certified? Does the candidate hold the required degree? Where and how was the candidate trained?

While prior training is certainly no guarantee of future results, administrators responsible for hiring do often turn to candidates' formal training and preparation as an initial screening mechanism. When doing so, one consideration facing school administrators is the potential (or, perhaps, perceived) differences in qualifications and preparedness between professional candidates who graduate from educator preparation programs that are delivered through a traditional face-to-face model and those who matriculate through programs that are fully online or hybrid in nature.

Less than a decade ago, determining whether an applicant was trained online was easy, as only a handful of institutions offered online programs, and those institutions were easily recognizable by name. Today, making the same determination is not so easy, as most training programs, even those promulgated by traditional brick-and-mortar institutions, offer some online components, with many being offered exclusively online.

Because of the plethora of training options available, deciphering what type of training model the candidate experienced is difficult based on the candidate's transcript alone: and hopefully, as this book will show, that may not really matter at all.

Despite some early perceptions to the contrary, online preparation does not mean "bad" and traditional brick-and-mortar preparation doesn't mean "good." As in all things, quality is where you find it.

ACKNOWLEDGMENTS

The editors wish to express gratitude to the contributors of this book for their diligence and cooperation as each stage of the book unfolded. The interest of each contributor in providing and delivering a quality online education is what made this book possible.

Furthermore, the editors would be remiss without extending their gratitude to a retired colleague and good friend, Dr. Ralph Marshall, for his contributions at the very beginning of this research project. Initially, it was his curiosity on the subject that brought this book idea to the attention of the publisher.

Both editors extend appreciation to Stephen F. Austin State University and the James I. Perkins College of Education for the opportunity and support to teach online graduate-level courses to aspiring administrators.

Lastly, the editors would like to acknowledge the continued support given by their spouses, Dr. John Allen Hendricks and Dr. Jennifer Bailey.

INTRODUCTION

This book was written to give practicing administrators, human resources professionals, and teachers and students in university educational preparation programs insights into the continuous development of quality online training components.

In order to have successful teachers and administrators, educator preparation programs, regardless of the delivery method, should be of high quality. As more and more preparation programs are offering degrees and certifications online, practicing administrators need to be aware of the components included in a quality online program. This book will offer views and perspectives of online programs and describe components that are vital to a quality online program.

Additionally, online education, which began largely as a phenomenon in higher education, is quickly making its way into elementary and secondary education. Consideration will be given to online education in the PK–12 setting, since the same teachers and administrators who were potentially trained online (or not!) will soon be grappling with online education in their own schools.

STRUCTURE OF THE BOOK

Each chapter of *Preparing Educators for Online Learning: A Careful Look at the Components and How to Assess Their Value* will present the authors' perspectives and experiences regarding online programs. Additionally, the authors will include a discussion of research related to the development and growth of online classes and programs in general and those programs that are now preparing educational teachers and leaders.

The book is divided into four sections, each comprising three related chapters. Part I provides a broad overview of online education. Specifically, chapter 1 begins with a discussion of the three primary modes for instructional delivery used today—face-to-face, online, and hybrid—as understanding the differences between models is crucial moving forward. Chapter 2 addresses four of the most common concerns related to online learning, while chapter 3 broadly explores the research related to the effectiveness of online education.

Part II narrows the focus to a few specific issues that are proving germane as online education continues to develop. In particular, chapter 4 examines how and why the types of assignments and assessments that online students complete matter. Chapter 5 delves into the issue of student dispositions, and why accounting for those dispositions is important, especially online. Finally, chapter 6 relates the critical role that field-based experiences play in education, particularly online.

Part III attempts to add a personal touch to the development of online education by relating some firsthand experiences of those involved in online education. Chapter 7 relates the experiences of an online student, recounting her time both in and after completing an online training program. Chapter 8 relates the experiences of an online professor, transitioning from traditional face-to-face teaching to online teaching. And chapter 9 relates the experiences of working principals and human resources officers as they work through the process of finding the very best candidates for their schools.

Finally, part IV wraps up the process by exploring how the online movement extends to and affects other areas. Chapter 10 demonstrates the sweeping effects online education is having on institutions of higher education, especially in terms of policies, practices, and finances. Chapter 11 identifies the most desirable qualities possessed by candidates who were trained online, and how to identify them. Finally, chapter 12 brings the discussion of online education forward to demonstrate how it is already beginning to impact K–12 education.

Part I

Overview of Online Programs

I

TEACHING AND LEARNING

How It's Done

Beth Gound

As the variety in training and preparation options for preservice teachers and administrators increases, those responsible for hiring new teachers and administrators may want to begin—if they have not already—reviewing the quality of the applicants' preparation and training programs. To do that, understanding the three major instructional delivery methods through which that training can occur and that are currently being utilized in preparation programs is vital.

TRAINING MODELS

Ever since the ancient Greeks began formalizing education, teachers have searched for more effective practices to deliver content and engage their students in the learning process. Typically those instructional practices develop within the classroom, but over time, learning has been seeping out of the classroom and into other formats, where teachers and students are not always connected by time and space. Today, most formal learning, especially in terms of educator preparation, occurs through one of three formats, or models; namely, face-to-face, online, and hybrid modes of delivery. Each of these will be discussed below.

The Face-to-Face Model

The face-to-face (or FtF) model is the most common, most familiar, and most comfortable model; it's the traditional way schooling has happened since Plato and Socrates. Face-to-face environments have been at the forefront of education for over 500 years as the traditional method of instruction; teachers are familiar with the inside of classrooms and have developed routines and order to their lesson presentations, curricula, and classroom activities.

This method is often referred to as "same time, same place" since the instructor and student are in the same location at the same time during each meeting (Redmond, 2011, p. 1051), with sessions held either on campus or at a remote off-campus site.

Face-to-Face Characteristics

In traditional face-to-face environments, there is a set time and place for the course to meet with little or no change. As such, learning is only an option if the instructor's schedule and the student's schedule coincide. Almost all communication, between both instructors and students, is usually during class time, or immediately before or after class, though some communication may be made via email as far as announcements and reminders.

Class time is generally occupied with lectures by the instructor, who controls most of the conversation; small-group projects and discussion groups; presentations by students of papers they have written; viewing of various videos; and some form of paper-and-pencil tests. Depending on the course, the time, and the organization, class sizes can vary from 10 students in a small intimate gathering with tables made for collaborative learning, to hundreds of students in a large theater-style classroom with rows of desks for more lecture-driven lessons.

Personalized interaction may or may not be built into the model. As the course develops over the semester, it is up to the instructor, if he or she chooses to do so, to take the time to get to know the students, either through "get to know you" activities, out-of-class activities like games and school events, or other venues such as student organizations and extracurricular groups.

Face-to-Face Teacher/Student Roles

Often, the role of teacher is portrayed as the wise leader, lecturer, and all-around facilitator of information—the gatekeeper, if you will—charged with passing on his or her knowledge of the subject to the students. Students, on the other hand, are passive listeners, eager recipients of knowledge and wisdom, with little or no time for reflection or conversation.

For centuries, this portrayal was, indeed, accurate, because aside from telling, the means of knowledge transmission were meager and limited. If you wanted to learn something new, someone had to tell it to you. As knowledge became more readily available—and now pervasive—the role of the teacher needed to shift.

In response, many face-to-face instructors have developed and transitioned their classes so the students take a more active role in distributing information among their peers in the form of presentations, lessons, and lectures.

Concerns affecting the classroom atmosphere are the teacher's mode of instruction and workload. Face-to-face classes are mostly geared with discussions and individual, paired, and group activities that involve hours of preparation for the 45–90-minute sessions.

During the face-to-face interaction, discussions can turn into debates, students who miss scheduled class time require makeup notes or makeup work, and, depending on the location, the drive can create a time crunch for those who live far away from the campus.

The Online Model

Online instruction was born in the combination of the ideas of distance learning and the acquisition of knowledge through the use of audiovisual aids and computers. Distance learning started as early as the 1700s, with letter writing and correspondence, and as a means for those students who could not attend traditional classroom instruction.

Technological advances through the first half of the 20th century led to many innovations in distance education, such as the use of radio and television broadcasting, telephone-based formats, and televised courses. Most recently, the Internet is transforming distance education, becoming the main channel for distance learning in the 1990s and beyond.

Online technology continues to explode in terms of development capabilities, and has led to online learning becoming established as a preferred method of delivery for educational content; over 32% of students—6.7 million—in the United States took at least one online class in the fall of 2011 (Miller, 2014).

Online Characteristics

In an online "classroom," issues of coincidental time and space disappear. There is no longer a need for students and teacher to be in the same place at the same time, hence online learning is commonly referenced as "anytime, anywhere." Access to learning is widened, since more students can commit to study who would otherwise be limited geographically or through work and life obligations.

Each online course is developed, housed, and delivered in some type of course management software that controls all aspects of that course, including content delivery, assessment, and communication. It's the instructor's responsibility to build the course within this system, and it's the instructor's opportunity (and responsibility) to showcase his or her teaching skills by creating a course that is meaningful and engaging.

When learning online, contrary to common perception, teacher/student communication is often enhanced, becoming more frequent and more personalized. Communication primarily occurs through tools that are a part of the course management system.

Just as in a face-to-face classroom meeting, it is up to the instructor to develop professional relationships within the class, including instructor-to-student, student-to-student, and student-to-content. Just as community can be built in a classroom, community can also develop in an online classroom: people do it all the time in their personal lives through social media!

But within this community, online learning also presents a sense of anonymity, which has typically been identified as a positive attribute of fully online courses. In an online class, no one knows what you look like or sound like, unless you choose to let them.

Additionally, students who are shy, introverted, or lack confidence can freely and fully participate online since the "fear factors" that inhibit them in a traditional classroom fall away. If an instructor's goal is for students to engage with the content of the course, then online learning presents a unique opportunity to do so since the classroom-based social barriers that limit engagement disappear.

Interaction can be in the form of discussions and group chats, usually conducted within an assignment or activity. Assignments are completed through the course management system and submitted in a folder or drop box there. Self-motivation is critical for students enrolled in an online course; without organization and self-discipline, work could suffer without continued face-to-face support from an instructor or peers.

A possible benefit of having no shared physical space or time is the amount of students that can be enrolled in an online course, but need for caution exists here. Due to the one-on-one nature of much of the communication, online teaching becomes more time intensive than traditional face-to-face instruction. Online teachers may enjoy the "luxury" of no defined class meetings, but that time is more than offset by the time spent emailing or talking to students.

As with anything, online learning presents some valid concerns. For one, instructors have less control and oversight of what students actually do. Students can easily ignore the written instructions, rushing through the material and not completing the assignments with fidelity or quality, just as they can in a conventional classroom.

Sometimes electronic discussions become discontinuous, almost statically paced, where there is no in-depth analysis of a topic, although it can be picked up again because it is on record. Also, with online discussions, there is no tone, body language, or eye contact with people in the conversation; therefore, misinterpretation of intended meaning can proliferate.

Still, the onus of responsibility is on the student, and that fact in itself makes a successful online student worth a look for an employer. In fact, much to the surprise of many students, the rigor and interactions of the traditional classroom can be maintained online, and in many ways, rigor can be enhanced in the online delivery model.

Online Teacher/Student Roles

An online teacher has pedagogical, social, managerial, and technical roles (Rhode, 2008). It is up to the teacher to provide feedback and instruction, ask questions, and stimulate the discussion. Teachers should also provide support and set a positive tone within class communications. As managers, they will grade the assignments, oversee the structure of the course, and coordinate the lesson units.

Students have the opportunity to be anonymous in their discussions and feedback, but there is no escaping the actual work. Online classes have become more demanding than the face-to-face classes and students are now taking on a different kind of responsibility role: constructing their own knowledge, developing problem-solving skills, refining their own questions, collaborating on more assignments, and becoming self-managers of their time (Berge, 2000).

The Hybrid Model

The third instructional model, the hybrid model, attempts to combine the best of both the face-to-face and online models, by blending the two. The purpose of the hybrid course is to take advantage of the features of two different learning models and create an optimal educational environment. This is where the traditional student interactions, face-to-face, meet the 21st-century learner, online.

Hybrid Characteristics

In the hybrid model, students and teachers meet face-to-face a number of times, usually less than half the number of traditional face-to-face meetings, for discussions and interactions, with the remainder of the hours and content being delivered online. A common practice of these blended courses is for the face-to-face meetings to occur in the evenings or on the weekends, so that students can attend outside of the work week.

Communication is therefore allocated in both sessions, leaving the traditional meetings for the instructor to clarify information and answer questions from the students, for students to present projects to the entire group, and for testing. The online meetings utilize instructor lectures, videos, reading content, and small-group discussions through the online management tools.

Similar to a fully online program, students can work at their own pace while still having a sense of face-to-face interaction, which can create opportunities to develop a professional relationship with peers and the instructor in class. Class enrollment is similar to that of the online learning method, depending on the instructor and his or her willingness to answer emails, grade assignments, and handle the workload.

Students can review prerecorded lectures, access course notes, and interact in online discussions, where they might not be comfortable speaking up in class. The flexibility of materials and assignments presented in a range of formats allows for auditory, visual, and kinesthetic learning to take place, engaging all learning modalities.

Hybrid Teacher/Student Roles

As teachers have the option of deciding when and how often to meet, students can enjoy the combination of anonymity during the online learning portion with having their voices heard in their face-to-face interactions and vice versa. The teacher is still the lead lecturer, although he or she has the ability to become the facilitator and assign student-led discussions, presentations, and reflections. Since part of the class is online, there are still the components of the teacher's pedagogical, social, managerial, and technical roles as in a fully online course.

Students have some flexibility in their meeting time, feedback participation, and coursework so that they are meeting deadlines for assignments and discussions, although without the constraints of a face-to-face meeting. For online or hybrid courses, it is important that the course designer create an easy-to-navigate module that downloads quickly and includes only the most fundamental information. Additionally, it is equally important to create and integrate dynamic and interactive technology components to develop a meaningful learning experience (Moore & Anderson, 2003).

MOVING FORWARD

The three primary modes of instructional delivery—face-to-face, online, and hybrid learning—have similar aspects, including teacher and student interaction, content and curriculum, and lesson preparations. The key is to have engagement throughout each course no matter the classroom space or design format. The responsibility falls on the teachers to ensure they are creating lessons that engage the individual learner through whatever medium available; the responsibility of carrying out those meaningful tasks is the domain of the student.

In terms of engaging students, online teaching can be more challenging than a face-to-face course, as the connection between the teacher and the learner that usually is present in face-to-face meetings must be cultivated in different ways. During face-to-face meetings, this relationship develops after introductions and as the course moves on; without those introductions and interactions in online or hybrid courses, those connections might not happen.

When considering how to create engaging online lessons, student interests and academic levels should come first; where are the students and what do they like, what do they want to study, what do they have to offer? Aligning engaging activities in online and hybrid courses should include social interaction, academic collaboration, and nonacademic social interaction (Journell, 2013), trying to create a hands-on environment that moves students beyond their computer. In a face-to-face class, there is that aspect of nonacademic socialization with friends and even the teacher, and online, without engagement in chats or group discussions, that socialization could be missing. In short, with added flexibility comes greater responsibility, both for teacher and for student.

The teacher must set an expectation of class discussions and participation for all students in each learning environment, which requires planning, preset procedures, and opportunities for interactions on the part of the teacher. Students who essentially observe the interactions of others and do not participate or give back to the classroom community are defined as lurkers (Rovia, 2000a, as cited in Journell, 2013).

If expectations are not set early in the course or in the syllabus regarding how many times one should respond or post to discussions or chats, these students could hide easily in the online course without that sense of social presence, or possibly, in the face-to-face, hide behind someone else physically. And with that, the value of the experience is lost.

CONCLUSION

This first chapter has outlined the characteristics of the three prominent learning models, as well as touching on the roles of both teachers and students in each setting. The following chapters will delve into these roles in greater detail, and explore more fully the potential advantages and disadvantages of the online model. Whichever setting students choose as their method of learning, most higher education institutions provide all three models for their students.

But as technology changes and electronics continue to permeate our lives, no one can pinpoint what online learning opportunities will evolve into. The primary purposes here are to build comfort with nontraditional educational models and stay abreast of changes within the educational landscape, both of which will be pivotal in finding, hiring, and retaining the best 21st-century educators for our 21st-century schools.

KEY POINTS

- Hiring the best candidate is critical.
- In order to hire the most qualified candidate, the hiring personnel must consider the program/training of the candidate.
- There are three types of delivery modes: face-to-face, hybrid, and online.
- Some positive aspects of hybrid or online learning environments are flexibility, anonymity, and lesson deliveries.
- Some concerns of hybrid or online learning environments are lack of teacher control, students doing the minimum, and lack of self-motivation.

REFERENCES

Berge, Z. L. (2000). *New roles for learners and teachers in online higher education*. In G. Hart (Ed.). *Readings & resources in global online education* (pp. 3–9). Melbourne, Australia: Whirligig Press.

Journell, W. (2013). *Online learning: Strategies for K–12 teachers*. Lanham, MD: Rowman & Littlefield Education.

Miller, G. (2014, November 10). *History of distance learning*. Retrieved from http://www.worldwidelearn.com/education-articles/history-of-distance-learning.html.

Moore, M. G., & Anderson, W. G. (2003). *Handbook of distance education*. Mahwah, NJ: Lawrence Erlbaum Associates, Inc.

Redmond, P. (2011). From face-to-face teaching to online teaching: Pedagogical transitions. In Proceedings ASCILITE 2011: 28th annual conference of the Australasian society for computers in learning in tertiary education: Changing demands, changing directions (pp. 1050–1060). Australasian Society for Computers in Learning in Tertiary Education (ASCILITE).

Rhode, J. (2008). *Roles and responsibilities of the online instructor*. [PowerPoint slides]. Rockford, IL: Faculty Development and Instructional Design Center. Retrieved from http://www.slideshare.net/jrhode/roles-and-responsibilities-of-the-online-instructor.

2

PERCEPTIONS AND CONCERNS RELATED TO ONLINE LEARNING

Stacy Hendricks and Scott Bailey

One purpose of this book is to dispel concerns and clear up possible misconceptions related to online learning. The pros and cons, advantages and disadvantages, of online learning will be discussed thoroughly throughout the following chapters, but in order to ameliorate any negative feelings related to online coursework and learning, laying out exactly what those concerns are is imperative.

And since the focus of this book is on preparing educators who will, presumably, be looking for jobs, the first place to look for potential concerns would be with those responsible for hiring them (a group that will be more thoroughly covered in chapter 9). For now, we will consider the top four commonly expressed concerns related to online teaching and learning.

DIPLOMA MILLS

Probably the primary concern commonly voiced in relation to online learning is that the courses are just too easy, with the "ease" attributable to low-quality coursework and instruction. At one time the concern over quality was—and in some cases it still is!—a valid one. However, it's important to note that this concern can undoubtedly be traced to the existence of early online diploma mills, created solely for the purpose of offering degrees at a very cheap price (though sometimes expensive) to students looking for credentials without the effort of rigorous study.

Granted, these diploma mills predate the advent of online coursework, existing in the form of correspondence courses and dubious overseas institutions long before the Internet was imagined. That said, the current suspicion of online venues remains well founded due to the ease of constructing elaborate web pages that lend any potentially fraudulent providers a look of legitimacy.

One can sort out diploma mills and illegitimate providers from legitimate educational providers by checking for an accrediting institution. Diploma mills either fail to publicize an accrediting agency or use a fraudulent one, which can be checked against the U.S. Department of Education's list of legitimate accrediting organizations.

Another way to check is by looking at the registration information on the school's website. Diploma mills typically use third-party companies for student registration rather than giving the school's mailing address. There is also a lack of selectivity in the screening process for prospective students, with no requirement for demonstrated success of the student in previous academic efforts, such as a minimum undergraduate grade point average or a qualifying score on a national exam such as the Graduate Record Exam (GRE), in order for the student to be considered for acceptance into the institution's graduate school and program.

Finally, most quality online graduate programs will require some form of interview process for each applicant, along with a writing sample, to assess the applicant's ability to communicate well within both verbal and written formats.

LOW-QUALITY PREPARATION

One early study (Richardson, McLeod, & Dikkers, 2011) indicated that those who are responsible for hiring campus-level administrators are hesitant to consider candidates who have received their preparation coursework online. The authors of that study surveyed 105 school district human resources directors whose responses revealed a general reluctance to hire principal candidates with online-only credentials. These candidates were viewed as being less prepared for the position than those with traditional credentials and would be screened differently in the interview process, primarily because the interviewers perceived the online courses as less rigorous, of lower quality, and unable to adequately prepare candidates for state-specific issues.

Additionally, the survey results indicated that most districts choosing candidates with online credentials as their principal would require some form of "on-the-job" training or mentoring that would not be expected of those with traditional degrees. At some level, whether these human resources officials' perceptions were accurate or not is immaterial, as their perceptions translated into reality for prospective principals in those districts.

Much has changed in the world of online education since that study was completed just five years ago. As subsequent chapters will show, the rigor and quality of online coursework is dependent entirely on the instructor of the course and the standards of the provider.

Like face-to-face courses, online courses can be rigorous and meaningful; also, just like face-to-face courses, online courses can be fluff and nonsense. As has been the case in every classroom across time, whether that classroom is boxed in brick walls or is an ephemeral reality extant only in cyberspace, the teacher responsible for that classroom is the final arbiter of quality.

Additionally, the "state-specific" concern voiced by the administrators in the Richardson, McLeod, and Dikkers (2011) study has largely dissipated in the past five years. Now, online providers are not just national for-profit umbrella institutions. Many public and private universities of all types, from large to small, obscure to prominent, have entered the online arena. In Texas in particular, and likewise in other states, many of the smaller regional universities have shifted to online formats in order to (1) meet student demand and (2) grow enrollment by increasing accessibility and reach across the state.

In fact, the authors of this chapter conducted a survey of all the public school superintendents in Texas. Of the respondents, 51% indicated that they did not try to determine whether a candidate was trained online or not. For this majority, the personal characteristics and experiences of the candidate were more important than the formal training he or she had completed. Moreover, those who did attempt to make that determination did so primarily to see if the online training was from an online-only provider or from a traditional brick-and-mortar provider that also offered programs online, with a preference for the latter.

ISOLATION ONLINE

Another prevalent perception regarding online instruction is that it lacks the social interactions that enrich a student's preparation for employment. Based on early forms of distance learning, this may very well have been true. Mail correspondence courses, whether printed or recorded, as well as early online courses consisting of text transcriptions or audio-video presentations of lectures, offered little or no communication between students and professor, with the exception of assessment of student performance.

Given today's powerful computers and capabilities for multimedia presentations and conferencing, as well as the option for hybrid courses (a combination of online and traditional), online instruction has evolved to the point of offering potentially more communication between student and professor than the traditional classroom setting.

Many students who would pass over the opportunity to converse with their professor before or after class due to time constraints, or for fear of "bothering" the professor with silly questions, or simply because of downright shyness, are more likely to use email, online discussion boards, and conferencing functions via the computer to access answers to their questions.

Professors have the option of communicating with the entire class via an announcement and communication function or communicating with particular groups or individual students. Synchronous interaction for the entire class can also be arranged by letting the class members know when the live chat or virtual classroom will occur. Most often, these times are posted in a syllabus so that the students can note them in their calendars; however, should a conflict occur, discussions can be saved as text files for students to review at a later time.

Additionally, in the online format, almost all communication between the student and instructor is one-on-one. Whether through email, text, videoconference, or just a regular phone call, the teacher is always communicating directly with the individual student, which actually hastens the "get-to-know-you process" and facilitates the building of relationships.

In terms of communication, online formats also provide other options that can be used to break down potential walls of isolation. One of these is the fact that with the use of discussion boards or chat rooms, when and to what degree each student is involved in class discussions can be documented. This type of accountability makes it easier to assess each student's involvement in the class, and encourage more involvement from students who are participating less. Thus, all students must respond to questions, becoming more involved in the class, and may not just sit back and let other, more vocal students dominate the class discussion.

Three other advantages of online instruction related to student interactions within classes have been observed by many faculty members who teach online. First, comments shared by minority students are more plentiful, because they often feel more comfortable in such courses due to less fear of being stereotyped or discriminated against in ways they may have been in the past. The format of most online courses allows minority students to decide whether to identify themselves visually or not.

The second advantage benefits shy students who have trouble speaking up in a traditional face-to-face class. These same shy students often become very responsive in class discussions in the written format of online classes. In an online classroom, these students feel they have nothing to lose. They will never see anyone from the online class and nobody really knows them anyway.

The third advantage related to student interactions within a class involves those students who may not process information as quickly as other students, even though they are quite intelligent and would have a lot to offer any class. Unfortunately, these students are often beaten to answering questions in class by students who process information more quickly. Thus, their attention span may possibly decrease in face-to-face settings.

CHEATING: WHOSE WORK IS THIS ANYWAY?

Finally, another concern clouding online instruction is that of cheating. Specifically, many believe that it's just easier to cheat online. Any student can find someone to write up a paper for him or her and submit it, right?

Student ethics is always a concern, whether in the traditional classroom or online, but safeguards continue to be taken when constructing online classes. These primarily are in the form of sign-in requirements; arranged proctoring for certain assessments; use of oral quizzes, administered one-on-one between the student and the instructor; or a student/instructor debriefing session.

These one-on-one sessions between the student and the instructor can be held through the "chat" tool within the course management system, over the phone, or through the use of another communication tool such as Skype. Additionally, assignments that require students to go out into the field to complete a task, or to submit an audio or video clip of them actually doing something, make cheating very difficult.

Additional safeguards that might be utilized more in the future to minimize student cheating in courses include the requirement of finger or handprint identification or voice recognition for students to access the course material and for signing into assessments.

Of course, just as instructors may not be certain who truly writes a paper in a traditional face-to-face course, the issue of cheating will always exist in traditional courses as well as those online. Teachers and institutions will need to continue relying on the moral, ethical basis of their students to help deter cheating within courses. More information related to student cheating is covered in chapters 3 and 10.

CONCLUSION

Indeed, distinct biases against online instruction exist. Yet as online learning becomes even more common, and as more and more school administrators and hiring officers have their own experiences through taking online courses, these biases will likely diminish. Because online learning is newer, we tend to remember the experiences related to it more vividly. For every "bad" experience someone has in an online class, that person usually forgets about all the "bad" experiences he had years ago in face-to-face classes. Remember your least favorite teacher from high school? Would that teacher have been any more or less effective online? Probably not. But in all likelihood, that favorite teacher you remember would have been just as awesome online!

Those who are more familiar with something are also usually more comfortable with it. For example, one study of the hiring practices for community colleges (Guendoo, 2008) found a lack of such a bias against online instruction when hiring teaching and administrative staff, which was attributed to the respondents' experience with both taking and teaching classes online. Since public school administrators may or may not have experience with online study, the preference for candidates with traditional face-to-face instruction is likely to continue until those without such experience become the minority. Unfortunately, any bias toward hiring candidates experienced in the more traditional face-to-face instruction and away from those with more online instruction experience creates the potential for passing over some of the best candidates simply because of the way they received instruction.

As the technology continues to advance and the use of online delivery systems becomes more common within all areas of education, it is apparent that the perceptions and concerns of online educator preparation programs will change. There may be new concerns that develop; however, many of the concerns that administrators and board members have had in the past will no longer be an issue.

KEY POINTS

- Legitimate concerns related to online education exist, but those concerns should be mitigated over time.
- Paramount importance must be placed on the strengths and skills of the individual, not the format through which he or she was trained.
- In online education, just as in traditional face-to-face education, the ultimate responsibility for quality rests with the teacher.

REFERENCES

Guendoo, L. M. (2008). Community colleges friendlier to online Ph.Ds. *Online Journal of Distance Learning Administration (11)*3. Retrieved from http://www.westga.edu/~distance/ojdla/fall113/guendoo113.html.

Richardson, J. W., McLeod, S., & Dikkers, A. G. (2011). Perceptions of online credentials for school principals. *Journal of Educational Administration (49)*4, 378–395.

3

RESEARCH RELATED TO ONLINE COURSES AND PROGRAMS

Scott Bailey

A common theme throughout this book will be reinforcing the notion that online learning is both currently prevalent and growing continuously. Comparing the most recent data collected in 2012 from a survey of all 4,527 degree-granting institutions in the U.S. to parallel data from 2002 (Allen & Seaman, 2013) indicates that the shift from traditional learning platforms to online learning platforms has been swift and dramatic. Consider the following statistics taken from that study:

- In 2002, 9.6% of students were enrolled in an online course; by 2012, that number had increased to 32%.
- In 2002, fewer than half of all institutions believed online learning was crucial to their long-term strategic planning; in 2012, nearly 70% believed it was.
- In 2002, 28.3% of institutions offered no online courses; in 2012, only 13.5% offered none.
- In 2002, 34.5% of institutions offered complete degree programs online; in 2012, that number had increased to 62.4%.
- In 2002, 57.2% of institutions reported that the outcomes of their online offerings were equivalent to or better than their face-to-face options; by 2012, that number had swelled to 76.9%.

The statistics listed here leave no doubt that online learning has gained a solid foothold in the educational system, and its reach will continue to spread ever deeper into the halls of academia and beyond. In fact, online learning is spreading into K–12 education as well as higher education. According to Kennedy and Archambault (2013), K–12 students in all 50 states will have access to online learning opportunities. Importantly, students in an increasing number of states, including Michigan, Alabama, New Mexico, and Idaho, will be required to complete at least one online learning experience as a graduation requirement.

Two factors are driving the expansion of online learning: convenience and cost. Because of its "anytime, anyplace" nature, students perceive online learning to be a more flexible and convenient option for their learning experiences, especially students who are fully employed and working toward a secondary certification. As more and more students turn to online providers, educational institutions of all types respond by increasing their online offerings to maintain and expand current enrollment levels.

Since the overhead costs of online programs are substantially lower than their on-campus counterparts, traditional brick-and-mortar institutions may utilize their online offerings to subsidize campus operations. Nontraditional and online-only providers view the lower costs as a convenient entry point to increase competition and gain market share, forcing many traditional providers to respond by lowering the cost of their programs. The newly lowered costs attract even more students, reinforcing the need for more online offerings and creating a self-perpetuating cycle that will ensure a growing demand for online learning options.

ADVANTAGES AND DISADVANTAGES

Though the growth of online learning appears inevitable, considering both the advantages and disadvantages to the possibilities of online learning is important. The Illinois Online Network (www.ion.uillinois.edu) serves as a clearinghouse for research, information, and professional development related to online learning. One article posted there outlines both the advantages and disadvantages of online learning, both of which are summarized below. The advantages include (Illinois, "Strengths," n.d.):

- Access: Students can access all coursework at any time, from any place, and they can work at their own pace—all factors that make learning more open and accessible to all. Additionally, factors that often serve as discriminators in traditional classrooms, including age, race, appearance, personality type, dress, etc., largely disappear in online environments. All of these factors "level the playing field" in terms of who has access to learning.

- Synergy: Though seemingly counterintuitive, the relationships and dialogue that develop in an online course are unlike those from any other learning format. Because it is asynchronous, all students have the opportunity to participate. Even students who typically would not speak in class can, and will, participate in the online discussions. Also, those discussions become deeper and more complex because students have time to thoughtfully consider and plan responses.

- Student-centered format: All students engage with the content in a one-on-one fashion. Posted guidelines provide general direction and outline course requirements, but students are free to explore and allocate their time to topics that most directly meet their needs. Importantly, students may also engage with classmates with similar interests. Multiple paths of discussion and interaction are likely to happen concurrently, unlike in a traditional classroom where the instructor guides one central discussion. Students can be engaged in three or four meaningful and protracted discussions on different topics at once.

- Creativity: The online environment gives students and teachers everywhere access to all of the resources and experts available in the world. The new Web 2.0 tools available facilitate myriad methods of collaboration. The result can be a fresh and dynamic approach to both teaching and learning that increases opportunity and interaction and encourages both teachers and learners to replace bad habits with creative new strategies that will enhance their efforts.

As appealing as these potential advantages sound, there are some possible disadvantages to learning online that should be thoughtfully considered. Those disadvantages include (Illinois, "Weaknesses," n.d.):

- Technological limitations: All of the apparent advantages of online learning disappear for those who do not have access to the technology to make online learning possible. But even having access to acceptable hardware and the Internet is not sufficient. Online students must also possess the technological skills to use the technology they have efficiently and appropriately. Additionally, the technology can—and invariably will—fail at some point in the learning experience. Thus, lack of sufficient access to working technology and insufficient skill with using it can hamper the online learning process.
- Students: The students themselves can be a potential disadvantage. Since online learning is highly self-directed, it is only appropriate for motivated, organized, disciplined, and engaged students.
- Instructors: Online instructors can, like students, be an impediment to the success of the online endeavor if they are not disciplined and engaged with the process. The online environment demands extra effort from instructors as they work to compensate for the lack of physical environment by creating an online presence that integrates students into the fabric of the course.
- Curriculum: Closely linked to the role of the instructors is the curriculum for online courses. A common mistake beginning online instructors make is simply shifting the materials from their face-to-face classes online, a process that often leaves students disengaged. Online curriculum must be relevant, encourage discussion and interaction, and foster student engagement. Building structures that accomplish this depends on rethinking traditional learning structures.

Considering both the advantages and disadvantages of online learning, the Illinois Online Network concludes:

> Today is a very exciting time for technology and education. Online programs offer technology-based instructional environments that expand learning opportunities and can provide top quality education through a variety of formats and modalities. With the special needs of adult learners who need or want to continue their education, online programs offer a convenient solution to conflicts with work, family and study schedules. Institutions of higher education have found

that online programs are essential in providing access to education for the populations they wish to serve. In order for an online program to be successful, the curriculum, the facilitator, the technology and the students must be carefully considered and balanced in order to take full advantage of the strengths of this format and at the same time, avoid pitfalls that could result from its weaknesses. (Illinois, "Weaknesses," n.d., para. 13)

CHALLENGES

The salient challenge facing online education is one of authenticity: How do instructors know that the students who are receiving the grade are the ones actually doing the work? As online learning expands, so do the opportunities to misuse it.

For example, there are companies, such as BoostMyGrades.com and NoNeedToStudy.com, that will take courses for a fee. But this is not a problem unique to online learning—companies doing and selling work for and to students has been more than a cottage industry for decades. Because online education is new, the problems and challenges seem new, too, but in reality they are not.

Online providers are moving to address the challenge of authenticity of student work, employing techniques as simple as requiring students to sign an honor code, as conventional as proctoring exams (either in person or via webcam), or as complex as using computer programs that register personally identifiable information or perform real-time keystroke analysis to ensure that the same person is the one doing all the work.

In fact, since 2008, federal law requires that colleges accepting federal financial aid for online students adopt and implement specific policies and procedures for discouraging and preventing financial and academic fraud (Marklein, 2013).

The reality is that overblown concerns about online authenticity have resulted in a situation similar to that of the "old school" teacher who refuses to maintain an electronic grade book because her grades might "get lost," never realizing that her paper grade book is much more vulnerable to damage, loss, or theft. It's a case of familiarity breeding acceptance.

BANE OR BOON?

As online learning continues to proliferate, the primary issues facing those responsible for evaluating online learning in a practical sense (i.e., consideration of hiring candidates trained in online programs) are the intertwined notions of quality and effectiveness. Quality refers to the inputs (content and teaching) of the program—does it offer what students need to know? Effectiveness refers to the outputs of the program—do students exit the program with the knowledge and skills they need to be successful?

Much of the current debate about online learning hinges on these two factors, quality and effectiveness, and as is the case with most issues in education, opinions range widely, with like consideration given to online learning as both bane and boon.

Some (see, as contemporary examples, Christensen & Eyring, 2011; Christensen, Horn, & Johnson, 2010) argue convincingly that online learning will prove to be a catalyst that changes the nature of schooling at all levels, but especially secondary and postsecondary levels. Or, as Horn (2012) optimistically stated, "online learning is a disruptive innovation that has the potential to help transform the present-day monolithic, factory-model education system into a student-centric and far more affordable fit for the 21st century" (p. 2).

The logistical and economical qualities attributed to online education will ultimately tip the scales in its favor and put irresistible pressure to change on the traditional model of education.

Those holding the opposing view (see the readings from Cuban, 2013, as timely examples) generally acknowledge that online learning has the potential to trigger sweeping change throughout the educational system, but that in all likelihood it will not. The failure of online learning to spark significant change will stem from the same source that has stymied so many change initiatives before it: systemic inertia (Cuban, 2013).

Changes in the educational structure seldom impinge on classroom practice because individual teachers can shut their classroom doors and effectively block those changes. Such may be the fate of online learning.

Also, Cuban (2013, June 7) argues that there is little viable research that indicates online learning actually works. The studies that are available, he claims, are of poor quality, fail to account for significant variables, or are otherwise flawed. Despite the growth of online learning, proponents will, at some point, be held accountable for demonstrating success, or the system will revert to the traditional model.

WHAT THE RESEARCH SAYS

Though some may call it "shoddy" (Cuban, 2013, June 7), examining the available research related to online learning is an important first step in evaluating online programs. Most recent discussions of the research base related to online learning reference a 2010 study commissioned by the U.S. Department of Education (USDE). That study was a meta-analysis (a study of studies) of more than 1,000 empirical studies conducted between 1996 and July 2008.

Accordingly, "analysts screened these studies to find those that (a) contrasted an online to a face-to-face condition, (b) measured student learning outcomes, (c) used a rigorous research design, and (d) provided adequate information to calculate an effect size" (USDE, 2010, p. ix).

Based on those criteria, the USDE sifted down to a handful of studies that were included in the final results. Based on that group of studies, 50 individual possible effects were identified where online learning could be compared with traditional classroom learning. Of those 50 effects, 11 were significantly positive, favoring the online condition, three were negative against the online condition, and the balance was neutral.

More specifically, the USDE (2010) found that:

- *"Students in online conditions performed modestly better, on average, than those learning the same material through traditional face-to-face instruction"* (p. xiv). Though the positive effect of online instruction was broad, it was not deep, and the report notes that the differences may be more attributable to pedagogical and curricular differences than the online medium itself.
- *"Instruction combining online and face-to-face elements had a larger advantage relative to purely face-to-face instruction than did purely online instruction"* (p. xv). The takeaway here is that some form of blended learning may be best, as the differences

between purely online instruction and classroom-based instruction were statistically insignificant. It was the blended situations, combining classroom experience and an online component, that gave the online experiences the overall advantage.

- *"Effect sizes were larger for studies in which the online instruction was collaborative or instructor-directed than in those studies where online learners worked independently"* (p. xv). Overall, students perform better online when they are either part of a learning group or directed by an instructor.
- *"Most of the variations in the way in which different studies implemented online learning did not affect student learning outcomes significantly"* (p. xv). Though data was drawn from a small number of studies, there was no significant difference between methods of online instruction.
- *"The effectiveness of online learning approaches appears quite broad across different content and learner types"* (p. xv). The data was not conclusive, but online learning appeared to present benefits to all levels of students. However, most of the students were postsecondary; the few studies related to K–12 students were less conclusive. Thus, at first blush, it appears older students perform better online.
- *"Effect sizes were larger for studies in which the online and face-to-face conditions varied in terms of curriculum materials and aspects of instructional approach in addition to the medium of instruction"* (p. xvi). Varying curriculum and instruction in the online format was important. In those studies where the curriculum and instruction were identical in both the online and traditional models, differences in performance were negligible.

Taken together, these findings indicate that online learning may certainly present a viable option for educational attainment. Though the USDE acknowledges throughout its report that the studies under consideration were flawed in several ways (e.g., small sample size, failure to control for potential researcher bias, failure to control for other effects), it is important to remember that these were the only studies available at the time.

Some subsequent studies have drawn slightly contrary conclusions. For instance, a group at the National Bureau of Economic Research

(Figlio, Rush, & Yin, 2010) concluded that overall, students who watched videos of lectures online performed moderately lower than those who watched them live in the classroom.

More recently, the Community College Research Center (CCRC) (2013) determined that students are more likely to withdraw from online courses, that those students who do persist perform slightly lower in online courses (with a 3%–6% higher failure rate), and that academically weaker students are less likely to persist and succeed in online courses.

A QUESTION OF QUALITY

That online learning is at least as effective as traditional classroom-based learning is really not surprising. After all, the online platform is just the *medium* through which learning happens. A seminal study by Richard Clark (1983) determined that the technologies used in education are "mere vehicles that deliver instruction but do not influence achievement any more than the truck that delivers our groceries causes changes in our nutrition" (p. 445).

Online learning is just another medium, another technology in a long line of technologies that *can be used*—but only with intentionality and planning—to facilitate and enhance learning.

Learning online is no different than textbooks, blackboards, clickers, desktop computers, overhead projectors, interactive whiteboards, interactive TV, distance education, or any of hundreds of other innovations that have promised to change education. And in all cases, the innovation is only as good as its implementation. Determining the quality of online learning requires looking at how it is implemented.

Mendenhall (2011) concurs with the notion that the means of delivery, whether online or otherwise, is not the determinant of quality, pointedly noting that "there is high-quality online learning, and there is high-quality classroom learning, just as there is low-quality learning in both settings" (p. B23). Echoing what other researchers have found, Mendenhall mentions that, despite the ever-expanding array of technological tools available, most online learning remains reflective of traditional teacher-centered classroom instruction.

Even though it may be offered online, the instructors do not leverage the potential of the technology. Instead, they design courses that consist of teacher-developed content delivered in a teacher-determined sequence over a teacher-designated time frame. Considering those factors, it is easy to see that the controlling factor in terms of the quality of the students' learning experiences is the individual teacher, not the medium of delivery.

FIRST, DO NO HARM

Taking everything discussed above into consideration led the USDE to the conclusion that "when used by itself, online learning appears to be as effective as conventional classroom instruction, but no more so" (USDE, 2010, p. xvii). Online instruction may not be better than conventional classroom instruction, but it apparently is no worse, either. Establishing that premise is important.

Looking at what the detractors say is equally important when evaluating online programs from the perspective of potentially hiring candidates trained through those programs. Taken as a broad stroke, the criticisms of online learning are actually positive as they relate to the hiring process.

Though certainly unfortunate as an educational outcome, the fact that more students may fail or not persist in online courses (CCRC, 2013) can be viewed as a positive outcome in the hiring process, because it can mean that online programs are rigorous and comprehensive, that students who complete them are self-disciplined and effective time managers, and, importantly, that they are persistent and dedicated to seeing a task through to completion, all of which are important qualities on the job.

Even as the prevalence and relevance of online learning shifts into mainstream media, the question of effectiveness diminishes in importance. For instance, writing for *Forbes* magazine, Tamny (2013) proposes that online education is a "bubble" about to burst. His proposition is interesting because he turns the standard view of education on its head. The higher education experience is about just that—the experience. It is about status, connections, and rank; it is not about learning.

Online education is focused strictly on learning, not on the more traditional experiences surrounding higher education, and, he argues, employers don't care as much about the knowledge and skills candidates have as they do about the intangibles a traditional campus experience offers. While all may not agree on what employers value, Tamny's argument can certainly be construed as an endorsement of the effectiveness of online learning, just as long as learning is the focus.

CONCLUSION

In sum, based on the available research, whether it revolutionizes education or not, the influence of online learning will continue to grow. Moreover, it is a viable educational medium with the potential for positive and effective learning experiences. Whether online learning is beneficial or not, it is, at worst, educationally neutral and that answers the question of effectiveness.

Online learning is equally as effective as other instructional methods, which means it passes the primary test often attributed to the Hippocratic Oath, to "first, do no harm." And that means the primary responsibility of employers is to evaluate *what* their potential employees know, not *how* they came to know it.

KEY POINTS

- Online learning has gained a solid, and ever-expanding, foothold in all levels of education.
- Online learning is characterized by a unique set of both advantages and disadvantages, but the strengths outweigh the potential weaknesses.
- Online learning, as a medium, can be just as effective as any other means of learning.
- The real determinant of quality in online learning—just as in any other form—rests on the individual instructor!

REFERENCES

Allen, I. E., & Seaman, J. (2013). *Changing course: Ten years of tracking online education in the United States*. Newburyport, MD: The Sloan Consortium. Retrieved from http://www.onlinelearningsurvey.com/reports/changingcourse.pdf.

Christensen, C. M., & Eyring, H. J. (2011). *The innovative university: Changing the DNA of higher education from the inside out*. San Francisco: Jossey-Bass.

Christensen, C. M., Horn, M. B., & Johnson, C. W. (2010). *Disrupting class: How disruptive innovation will change the way the world learns*. New York, NY: McGraw-Hill.

Clark, R. C. (1983). Reconsidering research on learning from media. *Review of Educational Research 53*, 445–459.

Community College Research Center. (2013, April). *What we know about online course outcomes*. New York, NY: Teachers College, Columbia University. Retrieved from http://ccrc.tc.columbia.edu/media/k2/attachments/What-We-Know-About-Online-Course-Outcomes.pdf.

Cuban, L. (2013). *Inside the black box of classroom practice: Change without reform in American education*. Cambridge, MA: Harvard Education Press.

Cuban, L. (2013, June 7). Online Instruction for K–12, Part 3 [Web log post]. Retrieved from http://larrycuban.wordpress.com/2013/06/07/does-online-instruction-work-part-3.

Figlio, D., Rush, M., & Yin, L. (2010). *Is it live or is it internet? Experimental estimates of the effects of online instruction on student learning*. National Bureau of Economic Research Working Paper No. 16089. Retrieved from http://www.nber.org/papers/w16089.

Horn, M. (2012). *Louisiana's digital future: How online learning can transform K–12 education*. New Orleans, LA: Pelican Institute for Public Policy. Retrieved from http://www.thepelicanpost.org/wp-content/uploads/2012/11/LouisianasDigitalFuture.pdf.

Illinois Online Network. (n.d.). *Strengths of online learning*. Retrieved from http://www.ion.uillinois.edu/resources/tutorials/overview/strengths.asp.

Illinois Online Network. (n.d.). *Weaknesses of online learning*. Retrieved from http://www.ion.uillinois.edu/resources/tutorials/overview/weaknesses.asp.

Kennedy, K., & Archambault, L. (2013). Offering preservice teachers field experiences in K–12 online learning: A national survey of teacher education programs. *Journal of Teacher Education 64*(3), 185–200.

Marklein, M. B. (2013, July 16). Colleges try to verify online attendance. *USA Today*. Retrieved from http://www.usatoday.com/story/news/nation/2013/07/16/internet-online-classes-security-college-courses/2518175/.

Mendenhall, R. W. (2011, November 11). How technology can improve online learning—and learning in general. *The Chronicle of Higher Education*, B23–B24.

Tamny, J. (2013, June 9). Online education will be the next "bubble" to pop, not traditional university learning. *Forbes*. Retrieved from http://www.forbes.com/sites/johntamny/2013/06/09/online-education-will-be-the-next-bubble-to-pop-not-traditional-university-learning/.

U.S. Department of Education. (2010, September). *Evaluation of evidence-based practices in online learning: A meta-analysis and review of online learning studies*. Washington, DC. Retrieved from http://www2.ed.gov/rschstat/eval/tech/evidence-based-practices/finalreport.pdf.

Part II

Quality: What It Looks Like

4

THE ONLINE LEARNING ENVIRONMENT
Quality Matters

Stacy Hendricks and Pauline Sampson

As the world continues to change, organizations must also find ways to adapt. The educational system is a perfect example of one of these organizations. In addition to many nontraditional students, universities and K–12 schools are faced with a more diverse population than ever before. Universities are searching for ways to meet the diverse needs of students as the student population becomes more diverse. Since technology has increased over the last decade, it only makes sense to look at the modes of delivery of instruction. It is apparent that administrators are faced with the challenge of offering courses in a variety of settings.

In the past, face-to-face courses seemed to be the only option available to those beginning their college career. Then, distance education became very popular. This concept allowed students to go to an off-campus site and use technology to view the professor and communicate with those in the class at another, distant location. While this certainly helped solve some issues, such as traveling, time, and expense, it still did not allow for flexibility, and students still had to travel to some degree. Thus, many universities have focused their efforts toward developing and offering programs online. The online method allows flexibility for the student. Online courses have also eliminated travel time and expenses, which gives back time and money to the student.

As many universities continue moving toward online courses and programs, it is imperative that the quality of instruction remain intact for online courses. Therefore, as professors or teachers design or redesign online courses, it is important that they understand the big picture. There are three components to the big picture: the professor, the student, and the individuals hiring the student. Quality instruction, regardless of the delivery choice, is a common goal of the three components of the big picture.

With many universities developing courses and programs online, it is important to determine whether the quality of education online is equivalent to that of face-to-face courses. Steinman (2007) noted that there are advocates of online learning; however, there are also individuals who believe online learning is a detriment to the educational learning of students. Regardless of the delivery mode, quality education for all students is a must (Steinman, 2007).

One way to determine the quality of education is to ask the students. Many researchers have done just that (Bailey, Hendricks, & Applewhite, 2015; El Mansour & Mupinga, 2007; Hendricks & Bailey, 2014; Leners & Sitzman, 2006; Mahoney, 2009; Muilenburg & Berge, 2005; Sampson, Leonard, Ballenger, & Coleman, 2010; Steinman, 2007). Additionally, there are advantages and disadvantages to learning online as opposed to the traditional setting. It is also important to inquire into the students' perceptions regarding their reasoning for taking one over the other. Two themes developed regarding the research of online courses: advantages and disadvantages.

ADVANTAGES

Many advantages were revealed when researching student surveys and interviews regarding online courses. Greater flexibility is one of the leading reasons students select online courses (Armstrong, 2011; El Mansour & Mupinga, 2007; Mahoney, 2009). This flexibility allows the students to continue their work schedule as well as time at home with their family. Students stated that this type of flexibility is much more convenient than going to a face-to-face class (El Mansour & Mupinga, 2007; Mahoney, 2009). One student stated, "Being able to do your work online on your own schedule allows me to go back to school while working full time" (El Mansour & Mupinga, 2007, p. 5).

When students enroll in an online course, basic content knowledge is not the only prerequisite for the course. Instead, a student must have some understanding of technology. As Baghdadi stated, the online educational experience can be enhanced if technology is used effectively (2011).

Mahoney (2009) found that student complaints about technology with online courses were few and far between. According to Muilenburg and Berge, of the participants surveyed in their study regarding comfort level with online learning, 67.7% (n = 715) are comfortable and confident learning online (2005). Hence, for the most part, students are at ease with the basic technology needed to be successful in an online course.

Lastly, online interactions and specific class expectations were also noted as positive attributes of online courses (El Mansour & Mupinga, 2007). One student noted, "Online discussions allowed me more time to reflect and prepare well thought out responses" (El Mansour & Mupinga, 2007, p. 8). Consequently, online supporters believe that technology interaction is the avenue that allows students and professors from all over the world to participate in the exchange of ideas, thoughts, and activities (Weber, 2012).

Regardless of the delivery method, the students' learning style should be the instructor's first priority. With the diverse student population, these learning styles differ immensely. Many students that struggle in face-to-face courses may find that online courses can be an outlet that allows them to take control of their learning experiences at their own pace (Asselin, 2012).

In online courses, students must be learning leaders. In other words, they must be active and take control of their learning as well as facilitating classmates in discussions and other group activities (Baran, Correia, & Thompson, 2011).

There are many advantages that students perceive as reasons to enroll in online courses or programs. Convenience, flexibility of schedules, class expectations, and online interactions are major reasons students enroll in online courses. Additionally, online courses provide the student with the ability to pace his or her learning.

DISADVANTAGES

While there are many advantages to online courses, there are also disadvantages. Many students have commented that online courses seem impersonal (El Mansour & Mupinga, 2007; Mahoney, 2009). According to El Mansour and Mupinga, "students felt 'the teachers did not get to know the students personally' and that 'there was no way of reading body language [from either fellow students or the instructor]'" (2007, p. 6).

Students also felt that they had "limited access to the professor" (Mahoney, 2009, p. 79). Moreover, in Armstrong's study, all of the students surveyed claimed that the professor was the missing link within the online course (2011).

If students view the professor as the missing link (Armstrong, 2011), then they also perceive concerns in other areas. For example, as humans, we desire prompt feedback. As a result, students want responses to or feedback on assignments in a timely manner (Leners & Sitzman, 2006). If the professor is perceived as not visible in the course, the feedback may be lacking. As a student acknowledged, "It is not possible to get immediate feedback as there are different time availabilities for the student and instructor" (El Mansour & Mupinga, 2007, p. 248).

Furthermore, if students perceived a communication gap, the students tended to lower their level of learning to a more strategic learning. The strategic learner tends to focus on the assessment process rather than the constructivist approach of actually finding meaningful connections to the learning and relating them to real-life situations (Armstrong, 2011).

According to Steinman, transactional distance "is the subjective measure of perceived distance between elements residing in cyberspace" (2007, p. 46). Steinman states that, as the transactional distance increases, the "interactive communication" between the professor and students lessens (2007, p. 46). Steinman asserts that campus studies reveal dropout rates for online courses tend to be higher than those for face-to-face courses.

Furthermore, Willging and Johnson (2004) found that isolation and disconnectedness may be two important reasons online students drop out of a program. Likewise, Muilenburg and Berge (2005) concluded the lack of social interaction was a perceived barrier to online students.

However, El Mansour and Mupinga (2007) reported online interactions as a positive student perception.

Lastly, while some studies found few student complaints about technology (Mahoney, 2009; Muilenburg & Berge, 2005), El Mansour and Mupinga (2007) cited technology issues as a problem area in online courses. The student responses ranged from personal technology issues with the Internet provider to university technology issues with the course programming platform. Armstrong (2011) added that technological difficulties were prevalent in online courses that lacked organization or structure.

There are advantages and disadvantages to just about everything in life. As discussed, online courses are no different. Academic integrity and high levels of student learning are two important factors when designing any course (Armstrong, 2011). In order to provide the best learning environment for students, it would be wise for professors to understand the students' experiences.

QUALITY COURSES

As illustrated above, there are advantages and disadvantages to online learning. However, regardless of the delivery method, quality instruction is required. In order to provide quality instruction, online courses must move to more authentic forms of education.

Beckem and Watkins (2012) suggested that "providing authentic, 'real life' experiences can be time consuming, hard to assess, tough to scale, and expensive" (p. 61). While these may be barriers, they certainly can be overcome in order to provide a top-notch education for all students regardless of the delivery method. Careful planning of activities can provide many outstanding, authentic learning experiences. After all, these activities determine the success of a quality online course.

The key to a successful online course is to offer a quality education. Therefore, it is imperative to address the disadvantages of online learning. For example, to address the disadvantage of the impersonal feel of online courses, Leners and Sitzman (2006) found that through personal email communication, online chats, constructive immediate feedback, and discussion posts, professors could eliminate some of the negativity.

Additionally, Wise (2015) indicated "a need to work with learners to assist them with establishing community or feelings of connection with peers and instructors" (p. 114).

In order to provide an online program of excellence, there are many available tools, such as emails, text messages, discussion boards, chat rooms, virtual meetings, and search engines. In order to provide a quality course or program, it is important to use a variety of tools within the online courses.

Asynchronous communication provides opportunities for participants to choose when to respond, allowing them flexibility on time and also giving them time to give a thoughtful response. Synchronous communication occurs at the same time so there are opportunities for dialogue with immediate connections and conversations.

The delivery of synchronous instructions is helpful so that questions may be asked immediately regarding any assignment requirements for clarification. Both types of communication have benefits in online experiences. Electronic tools are important in online programs for a variety of purposes. For example, communication and collaboration are possible through the electronic tools provided in an online course.

Information Resources

Students have access to many resources that may be used in their field experiences through technology and search engines. Many universities have their library services with online databases such as ProQuest Dissertations and Theses as well as many journals, ERIC articles, and government documents.

Google Scholar and other similar search sites can help students find relevant information quickly and provide numerous resources easily. Students can then share this information with each other as a great resource, thus increasing their knowledge base in an efficient use of time.

Additional information can be shared through webinars. This is often helpful when professional speakers or state department personnel want to share timely information with a larger number of people. It is more cost effective and allows students to access professionals from anywhere without having to leave their own work site or home.

Another way to increase collaboration among students is through the use of chat rooms, discussion boards, videoconferencing, GoToMeeting sessions, email, and texts, as well as social media sites such as Facebook, Twitter, and blogs. Students are very comfortable using social media in their personal lives so they are often comfortable using it in their professional lives. A brief description of each electronic tool shows how it can enhance a preparation program.

Chats

The chat discussions in online courses can be structured around new learning and practical issues from the field experiences. This chat sets a collaborative nature to handling situations so that students learn to support each other. Chat rooms can be used when students and faculty agree to a time and then use the online forum to discuss issues arising in the field experiences or any agreed issue. Questions can be extended to circumstances in the field.

Videos

Videos of best practices have been used for a long time in preparation programs. However, the ease of using videos has increased as students and faculty are able to take videos using their phones and then easily upload them to share with each other. Additionally, web cameras may be used to observe practicing students leading relevant activities. Web cameras allow guided observations where an online faculty gets to watch students through virtual observation of them in the field.

Collaborative Written Work

There are many ways to have students work collaboratively. One way is through the assignment of work for groups of students. However, if students are not located near each other geographically, then group work may become difficult, if not impossible, in online formats without electronic tools. Google Docs is one tool that allows students to share their work and make edits or changes that their entire group can see.

Collaborative Online Journaling

Online journal writing with students paired together during field experiences helps students look at each other's problems and questions and offer suggestions. This provides support for students while learning about the job. Additionally, it helps students develop a network with each other and a support system for current practices and evaluation of their own actions. Further, it can establish a support system when students graduate and become teachers or administrators.

Leading schools is a complex endeavor. Reflection on action helps students examine their own knowledge and practices. The writing of one's actions for another to examine encourages questions and dialogue to find better solutions as well as evaluation of actions.

The journals can be posted on discussion boards so that reactions and questions may be posted to further explore an action or issue. This contribution of issues helps develop a shared understanding so students can develop solutions and possible alternative solutions. This can help in the future handling of similar situations.

Self-confidence grows when students have support from one another as they learn about the job. This encouragement from each other helps the students explore potential solutions in a safe environment removed from the real school site.

Active Learning

The importance of active learning has long been recognized by educators in higher education. However, this has not always transferred to online courses and field experiences for preparing educators. Active learning requires the engagement of students with the material so that they interact in the learning environment with a larger variety of technology tools.

Interaction techniques may include simulations and role-playing, debates, peer review of work, interactive games, and writing responses. Problem-based learning works well to encourage active learning. It encourages students to explore and interpret issues to improve their own skills while examining multiple perspectives and solutions. Active learning provides faculty and students the ability to examine unique issues and thus facilitate each other's learning.

Discussion Boards

Online discussion and linked discussion lists may be used to extend discussion on topics or on selected readings. Students preparing to be teachers or administrators learn about real school problems through connections with school personnel and university faculty.

Discussion is situated so students participate in threaded discussions on potential solutions to varied educational tasks related to their field of study. The participation is conducted after students are presented with information and encouraged to analyze information and determine whether they understand all of the information.

Often, the discussions have trigger questions based on certain reading material provided online. Posting topics and issues on a discussion board serves as a tool to start a dialogue and a database on possible solutions to case studies. Students in the field can be asked to respond with an opinion or question related to the issues.

This then becomes a discussion thread that can be searched for common words or themes later, when analyzing data. This type of discussion gives students in a forum a connection to each other for contributing suggestions or thoughts while working in the field. There usually needs to be a facilitator monitoring and responding to discussion threads.

Case Studies

Electronic case studies are helpful for the presentation of real schools and leaders' efforts to improve those schools. This helps students understand the challenges as well as see potential solutions from outstanding educators in the field.

Major concepts such as decision-making practices, conflict management, organizational culture, and school improvement are chosen first by faculty and then presented to the students to improve the students' skills for leadership as well as problem solving while not yet working with their own sites. Students are able to explore issues that are a part of the educator's job prior to going into the field as a principal or intern.

Video Conferencing

Two-way Internet-based videoconferencing between the university and school sites are helpful in increasing the communication between faculty and students at their field experiences. Virtual field experiences can also link faculty and students to sites that are more diverse than their current sites. Sessions can be set up so that students engage in discussion with teachers or administrators working at a variety of schools: urban, suburban, and rural.

Portfolios

Electronic portfolios allow students to share artifacts that they feel impacted their learning and connect well with learner outcomes of the field experience. Individual students' accomplishments can be submitted as part of the electronic portfolio to show students' growth and provide authentic examples of their experiences. Further, faculty can include a required reflection on each artifact so that the student clarifies what he or she learned from that field experience.

Social Media

Blogs are one form of communication utilized by faculty. Faculty may present a short narrative on one issue. After this narrative is posted, then students may comment on the short piece either with questions or with further comments to extend the information sharing. Again, there needs to be careful monitoring of the blog because even though they may be closed to certain people, blogs still provide an avenue of collaboration, openness to use, and thus ease of editing or changing content. But professional practice can be strengthened by connecting learners to each other while providing them with narrative situations or issues they may not have experienced prior to becoming a teacher or administrator.

Twitter is another form of social media that can be used for education. Twitter enables students to ask each other questions either asynchronous or synchronous. Twitter is easily used as most students have cell phones and thus are able to access it for quick responses and opinions.

It can also be used as a tool for students to reflect on their own learning. Further, it allows the quick dissemination of information. Twitter does limit the number of characters so it pushes people to be succinct while connecting with each other.

Virtual Meetings

Virtual meetings are easily set up so that students, faculty members, and site mentors may communicate directly and keep the important aspects of face-to-face communication, but via electronics. Tools such as Skype (www.skype.com), GoToMeeting (www.gotomeeting.com), and Elluminate (www.elluminate.com) are examples of tools that offer face-to-face interactions in electronic formats.

Reflections

A reflective process is an important tool and can be structured in online courses either in structured and threaded discussions or chat rooms. Some researchers advocate written reflections on fieldwork experiences so that students can evaluate their own leadership of specific tasks. This reflection can also allow students to work together on solving problems and determining how to deal with real issues in the school as they learn to apply skills learned in the courses to real situations at the schools. Reflection can also be part of all coursework in the form of journaling.

The use of personal reflections gives students a chance to make their own connections to material as well as form their own perspective on the material. The critical reflection helps students explore their own understanding as well as describe the reasons behind decisions and events.

Technology Support

The best online experiences require some online support mechanism. Many preparation programs have assigned technology experts that can provide students, faculty, and mentors with online support. This online support should extend to field sites to ensure that the technology does not impede the experiences.

The use of the online tools mentioned above will provide a successful online opportunity for students. As the tools are used in an online course between the student and the professor, it is more likely a positive personal connection will form between the two. This positive connection may lessen or eliminate the negativity toward the impersonal feel of online courses. "It is up to the teacher to ensure an interactive learning environment by using approaches that engage students in the learning process" (Steinman, 2007, p. 51).

CONCLUSION

Online courses are certainly becoming more prevalent in higher education (Allen & Seaman, 2010; Kern, 2010). As noted, students continue to enroll in online courses for a variety of reasons. However, while the number of students taking online courses continues to increase, skepticism of online learning still exists (Allen & Seaman, 2010).

Consequently, it is up to the universities offering the online courses/programs to rethink the design of online courses. "Therefore, online education programs must be diligent in demonstrating quality higher education to both its constituents and accreditors" (Shelton & Isernhagen, 2012, p. 217).

With additional research on the effectiveness of online learning and redesigning of online courses, the online learning environment will be a win-win situation for students, universities, and employers. As universities continue to build online courses, they must continue to keep the student at the forefront of the discussions.

Therefore, while redesigning courses, it will be fruitful to consider the students' perspective on the advantages and disadvantages of online learning. Through a collaborative relationship between the students and the professors, universities can provide more meaningful online learning opportunities that more effectively prepare their students for the workplace.

Hopefully, with the increase in online courses and programs, a collaborative process will begin, which will possibly help professors understand the students' perspective so they can design online classes that provide the structure for meaningful learning opportunities that will prepare students to be more successful in the workplace. As educational leaders of the 21st century, it is our job to create a learning atmosphere that is accommodating to all.

KEY POINTS

- The quality of education online needs to be equivalent to that in face-to-face courses.
- Advantages of online courses are flexibility for students to access courses without having to travel long distances and thus take time away from work and/or family; access to other students and professors from all over the world; convenience; class expectations; and online interactions.
- The disadvantages of online courses are the perceived impersonal feel between professors and students; a desire for prompt feedback on work; isolation; disconnectedness; and technology problems.
- Quality online instruction requires students to have some content knowledge but also an understanding of technology.
- Quality instruction for online courses could include personal email communication, online chats, constructive immediate feedback, discussion posts, establishing a class community connection with collaborative work, reflections, case studies, understanding and planning for varied students' learning styles, and active/authentic learning assignments.
- There are many available tools to increase the quality of online instruction, such as emails, text messages, discussion boards, chat rooms, virtual meetings, and search engines.

REFERENCES

Allen, I. E., & Seaman, J. (2010). *Class differences: Online education in the United States, 2010*. Needham, MA: The Sloan Consortium.

Armstrong, D. A. (2011). Students' perceptions of online learning and instructional tools: A qualitative study of undergraduate students' use of online tools. *The Turkish Online Journal of Educational Technology 10*(3), 222–226.

Asselin, S. (2012). Universal design for access and equity. *NCPEA handbook of online instruction and programs in education leadership*, 140–151.

Baghdadi, Z. D. (2011). Best practices in online education: Online instructors, courses, and administrators. *Turkish Online Journal of Distance Education 12*(3), 109–117.

Bailey, S., Hendricks, S., & Applewhite, S. (2015). Student perspectives of assessment strategies in online courses. *Journal of Interactive Online Learning 13*(3), 112–125.

Baran, E., Correia, A., & Thompson, A. (2011). Transforming online teaching practice: Critical analysis of the literature on the roles and competencies of online teachers. *Distance Education 32*(3), 421–439.

Beckem, J., & Watkins, M. (2012). Bringing life to learning: Immersive experiential learning simulations for online and blended courses. *Journal of Asynchronous Learning Networks 16*(5), 61–70.

El Mansour, B., & Mupinga, D. M. (2007). Students' positive and negative experiences in hybrid and online classes. *College Student Journal 41*(1), 242–248.

Hendricks, S., & Bailey, S. (2014). What really matters? Technological proficiency in an online course. *Online Journal of Distance Learning Administration 17*(2).

Kern, R. (2010, April 15). How to maximize an online education program: How to choose a program wisely and succeed at earning a degree in cyberspace. *U.S. News & World Report*. Retrieved from http://www.usnews.com/education/online-education/articles/2010/04/15/how-to-maximize-an-online-education-program.

Leners, D. W., & Sitzman, K. (2006). Graduate student perceptions: Feeling the passion of caring online. *Nursing Education Perspectives 27*(6), 315–319.

Mahoney, S. (2009). Mindset change: Influences on student buy-in to online classes. *Quarterly Review of Distance Education 10*(1), 75–83.

Muilenburg, L. Y., & Berge, Z. L. (2005). Student barriers to online learning: A factor analytic study. *Distance Education 26*(1), 29–48.

Sampson, P. M., Leonard, J., Ballenger, J. W., & Coleman, J. C. (2010). Student satisfaction of online courses for educational leadership. *Online Journal of Distance Learning Administration 13*(3), 56–67.

Shelton, K., & Isernhagen, J. (2012). Examining elements of quality within online education programs in higher education. *NCPEA handbook of online instruction and programs in education leadership*, 215–226.

Steinman, D. (2007). Educational experiences and the online student. *TechTrends 51*(5), 46–52.

Weber, M. J. (2012). Hybrid course delivery: A good fit for education leadership preparation programs. *NCPEA handbook of online instruction and programs in education leadership*, 161–166.

Willging, P. A., & Johnson, S. D. (2004). Factors that influence students' decision to drop out of online courses. *Journal of Asynchronous Learning Networks 8*(4), 105–118.

Wise, A. L. (2015). *Factors that successful and unsuccessful community college students perceive as fostering and hindering their success in online learning* (doctoral dissertation). Auburn, AL: Auburn University. Retrieved from http://etd.auburn.edu/xmlui/bitstream/handle/10415/4540/Factors%20that%20Successful%20and%20Unsuccessful%20Community%20College%20Students%20Perceive%20as%20Fostering%20and%20Hindering%20their%20Success%20in%20Online%20Learning.pdf?sequence=2&ts=1430808959122.

5

MEASURING DISPOSITIONS IN ONLINE LEARNING

M. C. Breen

The Council for the Accreditation of Educator Preparation (CAEP) emphasizes the need for educator preparation programs (EPPs) to develop and measure professional dispositions in candidates. There is controversy surrounding the topic of dispositions, from their definition to their rationale, from their measurement to their validity.

The Interstate New Teacher Assessment and Support Consortium (InTASC) started the fire when it began the dialogue about standards-based, dispositional educator preparation. Then, in 2000, the National Council for Accreditation of Teacher Education (NCATE) began to use the phrase "professional knowledge, skills, and dispositions" in its accreditation measures.

With more EPPs moving to online environments, an additional layer of complication arises: How to measure an already gray area when faculty may not engage with students in face-to-face interactions? How can dispositions be measured when real-time classroom observations may not be included in a course? Is dispositional assessment even possible?

Principals articulate concerns about teacher quality for educators prepared in online programs and dispositional measurement in those programs: "It is difficult enough to judge the make-up of a teacher in a traditional program. I would be skeptical of how much we really know about a candidate's interpersonal skills and professionalism" (Huss, 2007, p. 27).

However, if EPPs are diligent about addressing dispositions in on-line formats, they can be sure to not only include interpersonal skills, professionalism, and other nonacademic characteristics but also have strong measures of candidate dispositional development and growth. Because principals have indicated hesitancy in hiring candidates who are prepared online and because dispositional topics that are infused into online coursework risk dilution, instructors must *explicitly* and *transparently* address dispositions with candidates.

This chapter explores the need to address dispositions in online edu-cator preparation courses, quantitative and qualitative dispositional measures, validity issues, and the challenges to addressing and measur-ing dispositions in online learning environments. Finally, the chapter ends with key features for effective dispositional assessment in online environments.

DEFINING DISPOSITIONS

Villegas (2007), using the works of Rokeach (1968), Brown and Cooney (1982), Katz and Raths (1985), Tabachnik and Zeichner (1984), Rich-ardson (1996, 2003), Tatto and Coupland (2003), and Pajares (1992), succinctly synthesizes a working definition of dispositions:

> Dispositions are tendencies for individuals to act in a particular man-ner under particular circumstances, based on their beliefs. A tenden-cy implies a pattern of behavior that is predictive of future actions. This predictive feature of the proposed definition gives teacher edu-cators some assurance that once program completers who have de-veloped the dispositions (or tendencies) promoted by the program assume the formal role of teachers, their practices will be in keeping with those dispositions. (p. 373)

Jung and Rhodes (2008) warn that part of the controversy surround-ing dispositions is the tendency of assessments that "focused on measur-ing characteristics of teachers (character-related dispositions) rather than competences as professionals (competence-related disposition)" (p. 647). Critics have argued that it is too difficult to measure the character of an individual.

As Villegas (2007) synthesizes the definition, individual candidates may hold beliefs or character-related dispositions that cause them to act in professional patterns (competence-related dispositions). A candidate may articulate a belief in social justice, open-mindedness, or equitable access to curriculum but until the candidate displays these tendencies in educational circumstances, the tendencies cannot be considered professional dispositions. This tendency, or action, can be measured.

Dispositions: Values plus Action

Critics of dispositions argue that teacher candidates cannot be assessed on beliefs, that the assessment of dispositions is too subjective to measure, and that an individual's value system is a matter of personal freedom.

This criticism represents an extreme misinterpretation of what dispositions constitute. Rather than being a value or moral system, dispositions are, as Villegas (2007) asserts, tendencies or patterns in behaviors that reflect a belief system. Dispositions are neither physical (action) nor mental (values), but both.

For example, a teacher candidate must hold the belief that all students have the ability to learn *and* demonstrate that belief in actions that reflect it. When assessing disposition, EPPs assess the actions that demonstrate dispositions, not personal values.

In another example, a teacher candidate may value collaborative work, but until the candidate actualizes the value through consistent activities, such as the creation of lesson plans that include collaborative work, the articulation of collaborative work as a possible solution as a piece of a response to a case study, and the design of collaborative work strategies in assessments, it cannot be considered a pattern or tendency and therefore cannot be considered a professional disposition.

Dispositions are not just actions. The skeptical principal in the previous section was wary, stating it was "difficult enough to judge the makeup of a teacher in a traditional program" (Huss, 2007, p. 27); however, in online programs there are *more* opportunities to gauge teacher dispositions because online programs can be more one-on-one, *if* instructors design them as such. This chapter will explore ways instructors can engage online candidates to provide rich opportunities to develop and measure dispositional growth.

Frameworks for Assessment

CAEP (2015) and other accreditation agencies generally do not define the professional dispositions they expect EPPs to assess; instead, the programs or units define them. Splitter (2010) suggests developing frameworks for "defining, identifying, and describing dispositions" (p. 209). For the purposes of assessment, EPPs should, when developing these frameworks, be mindful of the following when defining dispositions:

- Select dispositions that *avoid subjectivism* (Splitter, 2010) so measurements can be consistent and valid, but also so feedback can be meaningful to candidates.
- Frameworks must *avoid behaviorism* (Splitter, 2010) because faculty want to know candidates are exhibiting dispositions as a result of internal tendencies, not as a result of conditioning from grades or other program procedures.
- Defined dispositions must be *operationalized* (Shiveley & Misco, 2010). Consider categorizing dispositions in levels. Consider choosing a finite set of dispositions to measure: "To try to advance and measure too many dispositions would create a risk of doing nothing well" (p. 11).

These general considerations hold true for defining dispositions in both online and face-to-face educator preparation programs. Once dispositions are defined and a framework is developed, programs must develop systems for measuring the dispositions. Quantitative measurements are easily disseminated, collected, disaggregated, and analyzed in online environments and are therefore used more often.

Quantitative Measurement

Quantitative measures exist for dispositions, and could be predictors of preservice teacher performance but should not be used as a sole indicator (Harrison & McAfee, 2002) of performance. These assessments include psychodynamic assessments and are generally used to screen applicants for admission. EPPs, both online and face-to-face, often develop local quantitative, self-report disposition assessments using Likert scales or other measures; however, without evidence to support the measure, the assessment—while aggregable and easily reportable for accreditation agencies—has questionable validity (Diez, 2006).

Additionally, local instruments have been tested and have shown internal statistical validity, but do not have validity when compared to internal qualitative or artifact data (Johnson, 2008). Candidates and individuals can know *about* what to do for students, but when placed in a setting there can be discrepancy between knowing what to do and the actions candidates choose to perform. When synthesized with Villegas' (2007) definition of disposition, incongruence between value and action does not denote professional disposition attainment.

In one example, a candidate's self-report quantitative data indicated a value of a "caring and equitable learning environment"; however, that same candidate's qualitative interviews "describe a discipline policy where 'every child will be disciplined with the same plan'" (Johnson, 2008, p. 439).

As such, quantitative data is sometimes helpful as a tool to collect benchmark admission data to monitor candidate growth throughout the program, but it should not be used as overly selective admission criteria because (1) dispositions are not static and can be taught (Dewey, 1916; 1922) and (2) quantitative data is not always congruent with qualitative data.

While this type of quantitative data can be problematic, it does not change the need for measurable data to show candidate need or growth as well as to evaluate programs. It is not only possible, but advisable, to quantify qualitative candidate work samples in online environments to provide effective assessments of course goals and to provide effective measures of dispositions.

This is possible even when online students are not in field settings and when instructors do not interact with candidates in synchronous environments. EPPs need only ensure activities are designed to provide conditions within which candidates can exhibit the dispositions programs wish to develop.

CONDITIONS FOR DISPOSITIONS

Implicit in Villegas' (2007) definition of dispositions is a conditional claim: "dispositions are tendencies for individuals to act in a particular manner under particular circumstances" (p. 373). In other words, *if* candidates with certain dispositions are put in particular circumstances, *then* they tend to act in certain ways.

For example, when candidates who value curiosity are placed in classrooms with curious students, they entertain, promote, and encourage student questions. An oversimplified counterexample might be: when students who do not value curiosity are placed in classrooms with curious students, they may discourage or punish students who question.

If candidates who value curiosity are not placed in conditions where they can exhibit this disposition (a mentor teacher is teacher-centered and the candidate is not permitted to display the disposition, case studies are not designed to foster curiosity, etc.), then the condition has not been met.

This does not, however, mean that the candidate does not hold the disposition; instead, it means the candidate did not have the opportunity to exhibit the disposition. As such, programs must be sure to align conditions with disposition expectations.

To refer back to the earlier frameworks: if curiosity is one of the defined dispositions in a program, the program would have a framework that inhibits subjectivity (the program has structures that provide faculty with consistent measures to assess creativity objectively); avoids behaviorism (the candidate is not regurgitating or appropriating the eduspeak to achieve a good grade or please the professor); and does not operationalize definitions (curiosity is higher-order disposition and part of a finite set of expectations).

This disposition must also be assessed in a context. It is implied, using Villegas' (2007) definition, that action is a definite component of disposition—it is what differentiates disposition from value or belief. How, then, do online EPPs put this into motion? Specifically, how do online EPPs create contexts in which candidates understand and explore the dimensions of dispositions; create opportunities for candidates to apply their deep understanding in meaningful, authentic contexts; and measure both candidate understanding of dispositions and development of dispositions?

DEVELOPING DISPOSITIONS DEEPLY WITH ONLINE CANDIDATES

Candidates cannot be assessed on a disposition they have not been taught. This is not to say that they are being conditioned to respond in a certain way for the purpose of accreditation assessment—that is, after all, putting the cart before the horse and not the intent.

Instead, if the EPP holds an expectation that candidates value multiple aspects of diversity, the program must explicitly articulate dimensions of diversity and infuse this expectation throughout the coursework—not for fidelity to a research or evaluation model, but in order to deeply embed the expectation for candidates.

Unfortunately, after crest after crest of different assessment standards crashed on the EPPs' metaphorical shores, an assessment culture remained that left some programs with the notion that the standards would dictate the *actions* and *activities* of educator preparation programs. First, EPPs determine the expectations of the program. Then, EPPs teach it. This is no different for dispositions and no different for online programs. There should be transparency in the expectation of dispositions.

Conversations

In a program infused with authentic disposition development, candidates are invited to "participate in *ongoing, conceptually rich*, and *deeply reflective conversations*" (Splitter, 2010, p. 224) about dispositional behavior and the cognitive choices educators make before deciding to act.

Conversations can occur in online environments and are a necessary precursor for effective dispositional measurement. Learning management systems (LMSs) provide platforms for on-the-record, assessable chat forums, small-group discussions, and whole-class discussions. Such "conversations" can be formative or summative; they can be synchronous or asynchronous.

The benefit of working in online formats is that EPPs can more formally align discussion prompts to course readings that explicitly address the disposition. These prompts produce static representations of the interactions that can be measured for dispositional growth and development.

Holistic rubrics can be used to convert candidate responses to prompts within discussion threads. These ratings can be used to measure individual growth and development within a dispositional dimension and aggregated to analyze program development and growth along dispositional dimensions within courses and vertically as candidates progress through courses.

To ensure holistic ratings are not subjective and are not products of candidates writing what they think they are expected to write—a result of conditioning—ratings should align with the expectations in the framework for assessment. In that framework, the dispositions should be defined deeply with multiple descriptors. Additionally, not all artifacts that are assessed for dispositions should be graded assignments.

Conversations with peers provide a format for authentic dialogue and dispositional measurement—not course grading. As King and Kitchener (1994) assert, students can struggle with uncertainty and defer to "authority for firm, unqualified answers" (p. 54). While conversations do not provide the level of artifact that observable action in fieldwork does, and therefore do not provide the level of evidence of disposition, conversation is one valuable point of evidence to measure.

The objective of online conversation is to develop the disposition as well as measure the development. As candidates discuss the defined dispositions in different contexts, they form deeper concepts of the dispositions. In earlier courses, prompts aligned with a disposition would fulfill objectives to define and conceptualize.

In middle-level courses prompts might complicate the disposition with current events, laws, or case studies. In later courses, prompts might utilize videos of lesson slices of in-service teachers or other candidates and achieve more reflective objectives aligned with the defined dispositions. This type of alignment would permit an EPP to measure candidate dispositional development along a continuum of increased depth.

Written Responses to Open-Ended Questions

Diez (2006) offers open-ended questions for consideration for disposition assessment. These would include questions such as "Why do you want to become a teacher?" and permit candidates to use their own terms to describe dispositions; however, responses would be difficult to aggregate, may not be contextualized, and would be easily "scammed" in that candidates could give a perceived "right" response rather than an authentic response.

Similarly, when candidates are given a scenario with a more focused open-ended question, such as "What would you do?" candidates may not have experienced a similar situation and might give a perceived "right answer" that does not reflect the nuances of dispositions.

In the above-described conversations, candidates are provided a space to volley ideas and engage in the dialogic, enabling candidates to display multiple dispositions and growth throughout the thread and through the semester. This also reflects professional practice in that teachers engage in professional communities when faced with decisions—they "bounce ideas" off each other.

In individual, more formal written responses, candidates are afforded the opportunity to articulate thought processes and single-logic decision-making processes, which also offers insight into dispositional growth and development. However, open-ended responses, while somewhat helpful in providing dispositional measurement in admission, are not as helpful in measuring growth and development because individual responses may or may not reflect assessed dispositions.

This is not to suggest that open-ended questions should not be included in course activities or dispositional assessments. Open-ended questions *should* be included, as defined dispositions should be reflected in aggregate candidate responses if dispositions have been developed throughout the course of the program. Open-ended questions should be one of several measures. Again, responses would be assessed using the holistic rubric.

Case Study

Case studies can be used in myriad ways to develop and measure dispositions in online EPPs. They can be used to prompt discussions or open-ended questions as already described. Case studies can also be used for more formal analysis in dispositional growth development. One manner in which case studies can be used is to have candidates analyze a single case at the beginning and again at the end of the semester.

In Schussler, Bercaw, and Stooksberry's (2008) description of case study use with candidates, they clustered and operationalized dispositions in three domains: intellectual, cultural, and moral. Candidates wrote responses to cases that centered on the topics student motivation, appropriate parental involvement, and appropriate use of background information. Candidates were also asked to identify the teacher's values, responsibilities, and assumptions, as well as their own. Candidates again responded to the cases at the end of the semester.

Candidate case study analyses were assessed along the three domains: intellectual, cultural, and moral. Candidate growth was also measured in the ability to identify assumptions. There is an inverse relationship between awareness and assumptions (Schussler, Bercaw, & Stooksberry, 2008): therefore, if candidates have low awareness in the cultural domain, they will make more assumptions in this domain and, therefore, will engage in poor decision making. In coursework, initial case study assessment could guide online prompts for discussions to develop needed dispositions.

In courses, it is recommended that case studies be used to give candidates an opportunity to contextualize defined dispositions, identify potential assumptions, and imagine actions in scenarios candidates may or may not experience in the field. Case studies also give common space for candidates to analyze dispositions and provide controls for program measurement.

In other words, case studies can provide the conditions for dispositions to be displayed. Case studies are valuable because they emphasize the intermediary space dispositions occupy. They help make concrete this notion that "values are not just rhetoric, and dispositions are more than just outward behaviors" (Schussler & Knarr, 2013, p. 85).

Field Experience: Observation of Self/Other

While dispositions are more than just outward behaviors, observable behaviors are still a measure of dispositions. In fact, outward behaviors are the culminating measure of a disposition. Using only outward behaviors, or classroom teaching observations, for example, as indicators for dispositions is not advisable, because observations do not reveal the deeply embedded decision-making processes and foundational values upon which dispositions are laid.

While online students may be at long distances, teacher educators can still observe them in classroom settings. Candidates in classroom settings for student teaching, practicum, or internships can film themselves teaching lessons their mentor teachers are observing. Then, candidates can post the videos online—with proper permissions obtained from students.

Once candidates have developed the working definitions of dispositions and analyzed cases with those working definitions, they should have the meta-awareness to self-analyze and reflect as they watch themselves teaching. Voice-over narration and written reflection are two options for documenting this analysis.

This type of deep reflection would reveal the dispositions behind the teaching choices the candidate made and would be richer than a surface-level observation. The holistic rubric could be used again, keeping data collection consistent.

FEATURES OF VALID MEASUREMENTS IN A FRAMEWORK

There are key features valid frameworks must possess in order to ensure sound dispositional measurement. Qualitative data must be varied: a mix of assignments that includes online conversations, open-ended responses, case study responses or analyses, and classroom samples should be included. Additionally, not all artifacts should be graded as part of the course grade.

Candidates' work samples that are assessed for dispositional growth should reflect development. Samples that are graded might be skewed if candidates attempt to give a perceived "right answer." Additionally, instructors should give guidance in completing work samples, but too much guidance can cause the students to respond to the samples from the instructor's perspective.

CONCLUSION

Although dispositions and dispositional assessment remains a topic of controversy, it is a major point in accreditation standards. Programs that take time to define and describe dispositions, operationalize them, form frameworks for assessment, and design activities within contexts are able to create rich opportunities for dispositional growth, development, and measurement.

KEY POINTS

- Dispositions are "tendencies for individuals to act in a particular manner under particular circumstances, based on their beliefs" (Villegas, 2007, p. 373).
- Online programs should develop frameworks to define, identify, and describe dispositions. Then, programs should create assessments or assignments that provide rich context for candidates to exercise these dispositions.
- Measurement of dispositions should be free from subjectivity and not subject to behaviorist tendencies. Candidate work samples should be evaluated, but not always graded so candidates are not pressured to respond the way they think they "should." Online discussion posts and ongoing formative conversations are helpful formats for non-graded spaces for dispositional development.
- Quantitative measures exist for measuring dispositions but show incongruence in comparative analysis. Qualitative work samples such as online discussions, open-ended questions, case study analysis, and classroom teaching samples with reflection are assessed with a holistic rubric and are more reliable as dispositional measures.

REFERENCES

Brown, C. A., & Cooney, T. J. (1982). Research on teacher education: A philosophical orientation. *Journal of Research and Development in Education 15*(4), 13–18.

Council for Accreditation of Educator Preparation. (2015, February 13). *CAEP Accreditation Standards.* Retrieved from https://caepnet.files.wordpress.com/2015/02/final_board_amended_20150213.pdf.

Dewey, J. (1916). *Democracy and education: An introduction to the philosophy of education.* New York, NY: Free Press.

Dewey, J. (1922). *Human nature and conduct.* New York, NY: Modern Library.

Diez, M. E. (2006). Assessing dispositions: Context and questions. *New Educator 2*(1), 57–72.

Harrison, J. A., & McAfee, H. (2002, February). *Beyond standardized testing: Examining, developing, and validating the interview for admission into the teacher education program.* New York, NY: AACTE Annual Meeting. Retrieved from ERIC Database (ED471655).

Huss, J. A. (2007). Perceptions of secondary principals toward online teacher preparation. *Journal of Ethnographic and Qualitative Research 2*, 23–31.

Interstate New Teacher Assessment and Support Consortium [INTASC]. (1992). *Model standards for beginning teacher licensing and development.* Washington, DC: Council of Chief State School Officers.

Johnson, L. E. (2008). Teacher candidate disposition: Moral judgment or regurgitation? *Journal of Moral Education 37*(4), 429–444.

Jung, E., & Rhodes, D. M. (2008). Revisiting disposition assessment in teacher education: Broadening the focus. *Assessment & Evaluation in Higher Education 33*(6), 647–660.

Katz, L. G., & Raths, J. D. (1985). Dispositions as goals for teacher education. *Teaching and Teacher Education 1*(4), 301–307.

King, P. M., & Kitchener, K. S. (1994). *Developing reflective judgment.* San Francisco, CA: Jossey-Bass.

National Council for the Accreditation of Teacher Education [NCATE]. (2000). *NCATE unit standards.* Retrieved from http://www.sde.ct.gov/sde/lib/sde/Word_Docs/Cert/tprepapp/NCATE2000standards.doc.

Pajares, M. F. (1992). Teachers' beliefs and educational research: Cleaning up a messy construct. *Review of Educational Research 62*(3), 307–332.

Richardson, V. (1996). The role of attitude and beliefs in learning to teach. In J. Sikula, T. Buttery, & E. Guyton (eds.), *Handbook of research on teacher education*, pp. 102–119. New York, NY: Macmillan.

Richardson, V. (2003). Preservice teachers' beliefs. In J. Raths & A. C. McAninch (eds.), *Teacher beliefs and classroom performance: The impact of teacher education*, pp. 1–22. Greenwich, CT: Information Age Publishing.

Rokeach, M. (1968). *Beliefs, attitudes, and values: A theory of organization and change.* San Francisco, CA: Jossey-Bass.

Schussler, D. L., & Knarr, L. (2013). Building awareness of dispositions: Enhancing moral sensibilities in teaching. *Journal of Moral Education 42*(1), 71–87.

Schussler, D. L., Bercaw, L. A., & Stooksberry, L. M. (2008). Using case studies to explore teacher candidates' intellectual, cultural, and moral dispositions. *Teacher Education Quarterly 35*(2), 105–122.

Shively, J., & Misco, T. (2010). But how do I know about their beliefs? A four-step process for integrating and assessing dispositions in teacher education. *Clearing House 83*(1), 9–14.

Splitter, L. J. (2010). Dispositions in education: Nonentities worth talking about. *Educational Theory 60*(2), 203–230.

Tabachnick, B. R., & Zeichner, K. (1984). The impact of student teaching experience on the development of teacher perspectives. *Journal of Teacher Education 35*(6), 28–36.

Tatto, M. T., & Coupland, D. B. (2003). In J. Raths & A. C. McAninch (ed.), *Teacher beliefs and classroom performance: The impact of teacher education*, pp. 123–184. Greenwich, CT: Information Age Publishing.

Villegas, A. M. (2007). Dispositions in teacher education: A look at social justice. *Journal of Teacher Education 58*(5), 370–380.

6

CRITICAL ROLE OF FIELD EXPERIENCES IN AN ONLINE PROGRAM

Pauline Sampson

Many states require educator preparation programs to include field experiences. Further, some states identify the number of hours required for the field experiences in an internship with a strong commitment between the university and the school districts so there is collaboration in delivering a quality experience. The need for students to gain the skills to be educators is gained best through a quality field experience.

Components of the field experience may be enhanced through online tools. This chapter is organized starting with quality field experiences, including the need for field experiences, connections to the standards, criticisms of field experiences, support for and benefits of field experiences, partnerships with schools, planning field experiences, mentors, and new skills and knowledge learned in field experiences. This is followed by online enhancement for field experiences with online programs.

NEED FOR QUALITY FIELD EXPERIENCES

Students need to spend significant time in authentic school contexts working alongside well-prepared principals and superintendents to be adequately prepared for the complex leadership roles (Williams, Matthews, & Baugh, 2004). Current practicing administrators understand the role of leadership and their involvement in the design of activities to develop the knowledge, skills, and dispositions that are important for the students to learn how to be teachers or administrators. Students gain the advantage of completing relevant tasks while observing and participating with successful and strong mentors through field experiences.

The field experiences are critical because students need time to observe, practice, and reflect on the multiple aspects of the job prior to taking on that role. Olivarez (2013) suggests that the role of the school leader has become more complex because of the magnitude of changes required by the federal and state mandates as well as shifting demographics and changing communities. So educator preparation programs must find ways to connect coursework and critical aspects of the job in order that students better understand the context of the issues in their coursework.

Through field experiences, students can connect things learned in class to experiences in structured opportunities and then share those back in courses for collaborative insight. The field experiences give aspiring teachers and administrators a chance to learn skills prior to assuming a teaching or leadership position on their own. This practical component of field experiences gives students confidence when they become teachers and principals.

Additionally, the mentors in field experiences can help new teachers and administrators feel connected to the profession while also providing support beyond the intellectual support. This connection gives educators an avenue for continued support and guidance when leading a school and handling new issues. The strong mentor is available as another resource to share ideas on solutions when the students become teachers or administrators.

There is a shorter time frame to be successful when a principal takes on a new school, especially a failing school. In Texas, schools that are labeled "Improvement Required" for two years and have not improved will have their principal and faculty removed (Vaughn & Oliveras-Ortiz, 2015).

Two years is a short time and requires principals to have key skills learned in coursework and field experiences to make necessary changes. The importance of being well prepared for the principal position can't be overstated. This has led to many preparation programs redesigning their field experiences to have more hands-on relevant activities aligned with state and national standards under strong principals' supervision.

FIELD EXPERIENCE STANDARDS

Quality field experiences are meant to give students the knowledge and skills to be successful as teachers or administrators as well as provide them with networks to continue as they transition into the position. The knowledge and skills are important since the field experience is a required component of the licensure for teachers and administrators in many states. Additionally, one of the major standards for superintendents in the National Council for Accreditation of Teacher Education (NCATE) (2011) was an internship component as listed in standard 7 for advanced programs in educational leadership.

The standard for building-level administration with NCATE stated that the "internship is important and needs to be substantial and sustained with school based field experiences and clinical practice within a school setting, monitored by a qualified onsite mentor" (NCATE, 2011, p. 24).

The Educational Leadership Constituent Council (ELCC) standard elements elaborate that the internship experience should be at least six months in concentration of nine to 12 hours per week with the on-site mentor selected as an educational leader within a school (NCATE, 2011). The internship is to provide significant field experiences that allow the students to apply knowledge and skills from the other standards.

A similar standard was identified for district-level leadership, with standard 7 of NCATE stating, "A district level education leader applies knowledge that promotes the success of every student in a substantial and sustained educational leadership internship experience that has district-based field experiences and clinical practice within a district setting and is monitored by a qualified, on-site mentor" (National Policy Board for Educational Administration, 2011, p. 25).

The current accreditation standards also delineate the importance of internships and field experiences in the preparation of educational leaders. The Council for the Accreditation of Educator Preparation (CAEP) identified standard 2 as a clinical partnership and practice (2013).

The CAEP standard includes a strong component of PK–12 student achievement. The standard specifies "technology-enhanced learning opportunities, structured to have multiple performance-based assessments at key points within the program to demonstrate candidates' development of the knowledge, skills, and professional dispositions associated with a positive impact on the learning and development of all P–12 students" (CAEP, 2013, p. 1).

The emphasis on graduates' impact on improving PK–12 student achievement is not a new concept but is very consistent with the earlier suggestions made by Levine (2005) as one of the ways to measure the success of a university preparation program.

Current standards for school leaders also emphasize the connection of realistic experiences between theory and practice. The relevancy of structured activities is fundamental to strong field experiences. These relevant activities in field experiences are important whether courses were offered online or face-to-face. It is the relevant applications guided by successful practicing school leaders that create strong future teachers and leaders.

CRITICISMS OF FIELD EXPERIENCES

There have been criticisms of the field experiences of educator preparation programs. The criticisms have focused on the perception that new teachers and administrators are not ready and do not have the skills needed in their positions and, therefore, must learn too much on the job in their first years as teachers or administrators. They must demonstrate the knowledge and skills needed for school improvement with minimal exposure to failing schools in their preparation programs.

Another criticism has been that preparation programs have emphasized hours required versus the content of the requirements and activities within those hours. Well-designed activities that have real challenges for principal students needs to be the goal, not just required hours in field experiences.

Another criticism of field experiences is that a large portion of the experiences does not allow students to take responsibility and actually lead. Rather, students job-shadow others leading and are not given opportunities beyond this observation.

Students preparing to be principals need to have the hands-on experiences that lead to a clear understanding of the day-to-day activities of principals just as teachers need the hands-on experiences in the classroom. Some of these day-to-day activities most desired by students during field experiences are budgets (Sampson, Leonard, Ballenger, & Coleman, 2010) and site-based teams (Dodson, 2014).

Milstein (1992) studied the Danforth program and found that changes in preparation programs required a sense of urgency and asking school districts to partner with the universities so that the correct changes are made. This urgency is still needed today. Milstein (1992) emphasized quality internships with the field experiences "matched by changes and improvements in academic content and delivery" (p. 11).

The practicing principals who are site supervisors for students serve as the mentors who provide leadership opportunities. Student teachers have a district mentor teacher as well as a faculty supervisor. The field experiences must have sufficient time on task in challenging situations, with multiple field experiences for diversity and different aspects of teaching and leadership that are unique to different schools.

Others have also criticized preparation programs' lack of leadership skills training and limited quality faculty. Hess and Kelly (2005) and Levine (2005) criticized the programs in educational administration for not preparing school leaders to lead and transform schools.

Levine (2005) criticized educational administration programs for having too many part-time faculty who had limited recent experience and noted that the programs had inadequate clinical experience. Levine further recommended that many of the preparation programs be dropped. He suggested that the main reason for the poor quality of programs was the competition for students.

Additionally, the Southern Regional Education Board (SREB) (2005) conducted a study on 61 principal preparation programs in 16 states and found the following:

1. Principal interns don't get the opportunity to lead.
2. Districts and preparation programs are not working together.
3. Aspiring principals are undersupported during the internship.
4. Performance evaluations of principal candidates often lack a higher degree of rigor.

5. Principal preparation programs are out of sync with accountability demands.

The criticisms of preparation programs have been numerous. The criticisms led to many programs examining ways to improve their relevancy while also competing with each other for students.

SUPPORT FOR AND BENEFITS OF QUALITY FIELD EXPERIENCES

Not all researchers found preparation programs to be lacking. Margaret Orr and Robert Kottkamp (2003) determined that many programs for educational administration were successful and had strong programs to prepare leaders of schools. However, Orr and Kottkamp also suggested that, through the evaluation of programs for connecting leaders' preparation to effective practices, preparation programs need to address growing concerns that current leadership preparation models could effectively prepare leaders ready to meet the challenges of today's school.

The evaluation of the quality of educational administration programs started around the early 2000s (Kottkamp, 2010). Prior to that time, very little research had been conducted on the programs that prepared school administrators.

James Vornberg and James Davis (1997) studied preparation of principals in Texas using the Meadows Model and found that the internship should play a larger role earlier in the preparation program. Further, Vornberg and Davis found that the field experience activities rated the highest by the students were personnel, curriculum and planning, and school community relations.

Another early study was conducted by Megan Caldwell (2001) on internship experiences for principal preparation in Florida. She found that the most beneficial intern activities were in disciplining students, negotiating conflict, and planning/developing curriculum.

Further, Caldwell elaborated that field activities not conducted but desired by students were activities to help them understand finance/budget processes, designing master schedules, and interviewing/selecting personnel.

There continues to be benefits and support for field experiences. Students identified several relevant activities that they wanted as part of their field experience: budget, curriculum and instruction, master schedules, and human resources.

PARTNERSHIPS WITH SCHOOLS FOR FIELD EXPERIENCES

Educator preparation programs should encourage collaborative relationships with school districts as well as meaningful field experiences, and thus define effective teaching and educational leadership. The partnerships are readily connected through field experience designs.

More recently, preparation programs are encouraging partnerships between preparation programs and schools to design the coursework as well as the field experiences. It is important for a team of faculty members and current leaders who have mentored students to meet several times to commit to the improvement of a quality internship experience that would include observations, practices, and reflections (Dalton, 2007).

Field experiences should be planned experiences directly connected with effective teachers and administrators. These planned activities are most effective when carried out with strong mentors who lead students through guided experiences that stress learning and reflection. Reflective practices allow students to examine their own learning and gain insight from their mentors and faculty supervisors.

Practical field experiences help students develop the knowledge and skills to better understand and conduct themselves as teachers and leaders. The best field experiences require a strong working relationship between school leaders, university faculty, and students. This gives students a chance to learn and make mistakes while under structured guidance. Olivarez (2013) recommends that educator preparation programs design their programs for scholarly study of current research practices, guided field experiences with experienced superintendents, and networking opportunities.

The emphasis on the partnership helps ensure the relevancy of experiences, which was identified by Franklin (2006) as a weakness in educational leadership administrative programs. This standard increases the importance of the partners' involvement in the planning and constructing of experiences that are "of sufficient depth, breadth, coherence, and duration to ensure that candidates demonstrate their developing effectiveness and positive impact on all students' learning and development" (CAEP, 2013, p. 1).

One of the benefits of partnerships between schools and preparation programs is that students aspiring to be teachers or administrators can learn and practice skills under the protection of mentors. The experiences can form a network between students and school district personnel.

Additionally, the field experience can help faculty keep current with the realities of the demands of the job. The faculty, then, are able to design their courses so that students are able to practice the skills needed in the job. Current teachers and administrators must have a strong knowledge base of pedagogical techniques. Further, principals must know how and what works with their teachers in a shared learning environment.

PLANNING FOR FIELD EXPERIENCES

Any quality field experiences require extensive planning and coordination. Preparation programs must decide how many and what types of field experiences will be part of their program. Whether each course will have field experiences, a culminating field experience, or some combination thereof may determine how the field experiences are designed.

Administrative field experiences need to be coherent and sequentially built, with the beginning focus on practical aspects of leadership such as master schedules, budgets, parent communication, laws and regulatory practices, professional development, and appraisals. Then other field experiences should have an emphasis on instructional and administrative leadership.

When students learn about teaching or leadership concepts, the field experiences allow the students to apply what they have learned in the courses. Activities planned for field experiences should give mentors the ability to scaffold learning for students and the flexibility to change experiences based on students' needs in specific areas.

Further, there needs to be a wide variety of experiences planned as part of courses and as part of the field experience or internship. The experiences should be planned to include observation, participation, and leading in diverse settings (Dodson, 2014). Field experience activities are often dictated by the preparation program or the school districts, while some experiences should be students' choice in areas they want to learn.

Field experiences give students a chance to learn while leading changes under supervision. It is helpful to plan coursework experiences that allow students to examine real school problems and leadership tasks so they are able to reflect collectively on experiences and outcomes (Zubrzycki, 2012).

FIELD EXPERIENCE MENTORS

The selection of strong teachers and administrators in the field experience is crucial to the development of quality educators. The mentors must have strong leadership skills and a willingness to provide an experience that motivates the students to learn and grow.

The best mentors are successful educators who are committed, willing, and able to invest sufficient time and effort to develop the next generation of leaders through guiding practice and reflection (Milstein, 1992). Students involved with quality field experiences are more prepared and confident because they have practiced under those masters in the field.

The experiences help the students bridge the gap between theory and practice. Mentors can provide opportunities for students to assume responsibility for real projects that will help them develop the knowledge, skill, and confidence for leading.

Crocker and Harris (2002) found that the pairing of a mentor and an intern was a critical component of successful field experiences and the development of leadership skills. The working relationship between the mentor and the student is important if the students are to gain the most from the field experience.

Another aspect of improving field experiences is the provision of training for mentors (Wilmore & Bratlien, 2005). The roles of mentors need to be well defined. Since quality PK–12 school leaders who serve as mentors for aspiring educators are fundamental to the quality of the field experiences, then time needs to be given to the expectations of the preparation program. The preparation programs must locate schools and leaders that have high-level skills that match the preparation programs' identified skills and vision, as well as close proximity to the students taking the online courses.

The partnerships between university preparation programs and PK–12 school districts allow for the knowledge of required activities and experiences needed in educator field experiences, but also allow for the recognition of strong teachers and leaders in the field. Mentors are also chosen because of the emotional support they can provide students. This emotional support is important for long-term relationships.

Mentors in the field help students develop skills while providing them with support as they progress in their skill development. This mentorship often continues past the field experience as new educators benefit from continued support with their new responsibilities. Mentors also benefit from a sense of helping others as well as reflecting on the reasons for their recommendations.

Mentors present the current and real problems in schools and give students opportunities to practice with hands-on experiences to learn how to solve the real problems. The reflection of their actions gives them tools to analyze the results. This helps students acquire practical knowledge that cannot be developed in isolated courses with no field experience. Mentors are the major influence on the field experiences that ensure the development of strong leadership skills.

NEW SKILLS TO LEARN IN FIELD EXPERIENCES

Educators in schools today require skills, knowledge, and dispositions that are different from those required 10 years ago. Some of these changes are ways to adapt to changing demands, changing demographics, and changing standards. Additionally, there is more transparency amid higher levels of state and federal accountability. Specifically, the current demands of the principal position have increased the need for instructional leadership with a focus on higher levels of understanding related to curriculum, instruction, and assessment.

Skills are not learned in isolation. Olivarez (2013) shared the importance of networking opportunities for students to participate with many professional organizations at the state and national level to learn new skills. It is important for students to learn how to guide and lead others to a common vision and goals. They need the chance to learn and solve real problems that they will encounter as teachers and leaders of schools. The new skills require problem solving with others at every increasing level.

Self-evaluation and reflection are key skills for all students, and the field experiences can serve as a catalyst for strong educators to develop these skills. This helps students identify their own strengths and weaknesses so they can work on their skills with the support of their field experience mentor and university supervisor prior to continuing their own growth.

Students identified other skills they felt they needed as follows: discipline, committee meetings, instructional coaching, analyzing student data, conducting teacher observations and evaluations, site-based decision making, working with upset parents, engaging in comprehensive school improvement planning, handling personnel issues, and understanding school law (Dodson, 2014).

In order for the students to learn these new skills they need time and opportunities to "inquire about, plan, and enact solutions to authentic PK–12 student learning problems" (Perez et al., 2011, p. 226). Further, the opportunities should help guide students to find their own leadership skills and capabilities to connect problems with solutions that have the highest potential for meeting the needs of a school while collaborating with others on the solutions. The collaborative reflection on proposed solutions helps students learn limitations to the solutions, as well as positive outcomes and further questions.

There are many political aspects of an administrator's job that have become a larger part of the job. Aspiring principals need the skills to build collaborations and support team learning while in this political climate.

SUMMARY OF ONLINE

The students' field experiences help them gain confidence as they develop their own skills through the problems presented in the experiences. The design of online courses can be rigorous and challenging when connected with field experiences. Students then have a chance to try the solutions in the field, followed by real-time chats for evaluation.

Evaluation of Field Experiences

Standards such as ISLLC and CAEP are often used to review accreditation of educator preparation programs. Other ways to examine field experiences and internships in programs for principals, whether face-to-face or online, include asking similar questions to those advocated by SREB (2005):

1. Are the internships aligned with the requirements of the job?
2. Are the activities anchored in real-world problems that principals face?
3. Are principal interns given opportunities to first observe, then participate in, and finally lead real school-change activities?
4. Are interns working under the direction of an accomplished principal who can model key leadership behavior and guide interns to higher levels of performance?
5. Are interns placed in diverse settings?
6. Do interns receive frequent, meaningful feedback that lets them know how they need to improve?
7. Are they rigorously evaluated on mastery of essential skills?

These same questions would be appropriate for field experiences for preparing superintendents.

Principals evaluating their own field experiences while in preparation programs highly rate their experience. Many principals are satisfied with their field experience in their preparation programs (Sampson, Leonard, Ballenger, & Coleman, 2010).

Further, principals state that they could not be principals without strong effective principal mentors during field experiences. The largest percentage of principals satisfied with their field experiences were those who were able to choose their experiences as compared to those who had field experiences chosen only by their school supervisor (Dodson, 2014).

CONCLUSION

It is the quality of field experiences that is vital to help students gain the confidence and commitment for their future in education. Field experiences are needed whether preparation programs are face-to-face traditional programs or online programs. Observations, practice, and reflections in field experiences are keys to the development of strong teachers and educational leaders.

Of course, the students preparing to be principals must be connected with effective leaders in order to understand the complexity of school leadership; this, in turn, develops strong instructional leaders who know how to develop positive working relationships.

KEY POINTS

- Quality field experiences are needed in all preparation programs, whether online, face-to-face, or hybrid, for students to learn in authentic school contexts how to become leaders.
- Field experiences require time to observe, practice, and reflect on the leadership role so candidates gain confidence as leaders.
- Field experiences connect theory to practice with relevant activities.
- Field experiences connect students with practitioners in the profession for future reference and a network to help in the transition.
- Strong mentors are needed for quality field experiences.
- Experiences must give candidates a chance to actually lead and not just shadow a leader.
- Personnel, curriculum, and school community relations activities are rated the highest in field experiences for leadership.
- More activities related to finance, master schedules, and personnel selection are needed in the field experiences.
- Quality field experiences require a strong partnership between schools and preparation programs.

- All field experiences should be selected with extensive planning for types and sequence of activities as well as conducted in coordination with the site mentors.
- It is important to select strong acting leaders to serve as mentors who are willing to commit time to the candidates.
- Mentors should receive training on expectations.
- School leaders need new skills to understand change and adapt to the changing demographics along with increased accountability.

REFERENCES

Caldwell, M. J. (2001). *Educational leadership internships: Perceptions of participants attending the University of Central Florida, January 1993–May 1997* (doctoral dissertation). Retrieved from ProQuest Dissertations and Theses database, (UMI No. 3013885).

Council for the Accreditation of Educator Preparation. (2013). *Standard 2: Clinical partnerships and practice*. Retrieved from http://caepnet.org/standards/standards/standard2 .

Crocker, C., & Harris, S. (2002). Facilitating growth of administrative practitioners as mentors. *Journal of Research for Educational Leaders* 1(2), 5–20.

Dalton, M. H. (2007). Internship and portfolio for superintendent preparation. *National Forum for Educational Administration* 25(4), 1–6.

Dodson, R. L. (2014). Which field experiences best prepare future school leaders? An analysis of Kentucky's principal preparation program. *Educational Administration Quarterly* 37(4), 41–56.

Franklin, S. H. (2006). *Exploratory comparative case studies of two principal preparation programs*. Retrieved from ProQuest Dissertations and Theses database. University of Texas at Austin (UMI No. 3225408).

Hess, F. M., & Kelly, A. P. (2005). *Learning to lead? What gets taught in principal preparation programs*. Retrieved from ERIC database (ED485999).

Kottkamp, R. B. (2010). Introduction: Leadership preparation in education. *Educational Administrative Quarterly* 20(10), 1–15.

Levine, A. (2005). *Educating school leaders*. The Education Schools Project. Retrieved from ERIC database (ED504142).

Milstein, M. M. (1992). *The Danforth program for the preparation of school principals six years later*. Retrieved from ERIC database (ED355659).

National Policy Board for Educational Administration. (2011). *Educational Leadership Program Standards 2011 ELCC District Level*. Retrieved from www.npbea.org .

National Council for Accreditation of Teacher Education. (2011). *Program standards*. Retrieved from www.ncate.org/LikClick.aspx?fileteicket=zRZ173R0nOQ%3d&tabid-676 .

Olivarez, R. D. (2013). Preparing superintendents for executive leadership: Combining administrative, instructional, and political leadership theory with real-world applications. *UCEA Review* 54(3), 1–4.

Orr, M. T., & Kottkamp, R. (2003). *Evaluating the causal pathway from leadership preparation to school improvement*. Paper presented at the annual meeting of the American Educational Research Association, Chicago, IL

Perez, L. G., Uline, C. L., Johnson, J. F., Jr., James-Ward, C., & Basom, M. R. (2011). Foregrounding fieldwork in leadership preparation: The transformative capacity of authentic inquiry. *Educational Administration Quarterly* 47(1), 217–257.

Sampson, P. M., Leonard, J., Ballenger, J. W., & Coleman, C. (2010). Student satisfaction of online courses for educational leadership. *Online Journal of Distance Learning Administration* 13(3), 56–67.

Southern Regional Education Board. (2005). SREB report on principal internships. *Techniques (ACTE) 80*(8), 10.

Vaughn, V., & Oliveras-Ortiz, Y. (2015). Considering an overhaul to the new principal preparation program. *School Leadership Review 10*(1), 7–15.

Vornberg, J. A., & Davis, J. (1997). *The Meadows Principal Improvement Program: A preservice field based model for the preparation of principals.* Retrieved from ERIC database (ED444246).

Williams, E. J., Matthews, J., & Baugh, S. (2004). Developing a mentoring internship model for school leadership: Using legitimate peripheral participation. *Mentoring & Tutoring: Partnership in Learning 12*(1), 53–70.

Wilmore, E. L., & Bratlien, M. J. (2005). Mentoring and tutoring within administrative internship programs in American universities. *Mentoring & Tutoring: Partnership in Learning 13*(1), 23–37.

Zubrzycki, J. (2012, December 4). More principals learn the job in real schools. *Education Week*, 7.

Part III

Experiences Regarding Online Programs

7

EXPERIENCES OF AN ONLINE STUDENT

To Enroll or Not?

Stephanie Barber Applewhite

As students seek to continue their education or obtain teaching and principal certifications, they are faced with choosing from a variety of learning environments. The question that students should ask as they consider which type of program is best is, "How will this experience prepare me as an administrator?"

Likewise, a hiring administrator should consider how the applicant experienced learning and how the applicant transferred that experience into attitudes and beliefs that will impact instruction or educational leadership practices.

This chapter explores how one graduate student experienced an online, for-profit master of arts in education program that included a principal's certificate/license, and how that learning experience prepared her for the real work of instructional leadership. This chapter is written in a third-person format in which the author relates a story to share the benefits and limitations of the program, and ultimately how the student was able to synthesize her experiences into a school leadership role.

The author also includes the outcomes of the student's choice from a professional perspective regarding interviewing with principals and superintendents for administrative positions, and how she had to overcome the stigma of graduating from an online university.

AMANDA'S STORY

Teachers who are looking to become administrators are faced with several considerations when selecting the right program fit. Amanda had been teaching for five years when she began to explore which route would best prepare her for advancing into school leadership. Her desire was to become an educational leader and serve as a school administrator, preferably as the principal.

Amanda began to research different university options and realized that the online route was her best option for several reasons, but she wanted to be in a program that was designed to prepare her for the real work of a school administrator. For this reason, Amanda was diligent in looking deeply at her options.

At the time, Amanda's spouse was considering possible career options across the country, so she was mindful of selecting a program that would not be bound by a physical location. Also, Amanda needed the flexibility to meet the needs of her family, as she had three children under the age of 10.

The asynchronous learning environment allowed her to fulfill her different life roles such as teacher, wife, mom, and softball coach. Removing time constraints of class meetings and having the flexibility to complete her assignments online was appealing.

Amanda began to narrow down the search in hopes of finding a program that would prepare her appropriately for the responsibilities of school leadership. She began by identifying seven areas that she wanted to investigate with each online school. She formulated questions to guide her through the discovery process.

These same questions are answered using Amanda's actual experiences throughout the program and her first year as an administrator. Her questions serve to identify each section of this chapter and touch on the following concepts: (1) sense of preparedness; (2) online learning experiences; (3) field experiences; (4) types of assignments; (5) disposition development; (6) getting a job; and ultimately (7) doing the job.

Amanda chose to enroll in an online program that offered flexibility to obtain certifications for multiple states—that solved the issue of her spouse accepting an out-of-state position and allowed her the flexibility to attend to school needs and opportunities when her family was sleeping or otherwise occupied.

Once she was satisfied that her goals and concerns about the online learning experience had been addressed, she began attending online classes at a private, online university and completed her degree and administrator certification 18 months later.

PREPAREDNESS OF ONLINE GRADUATES

One concern that Amanda had was how she would be able to draw from her teaching experiences as an administrator. Also, she wanted to have more than a checklist of assignments: she yearned to connect her learning to her experiences as a teacher. As Amanda watched the administrators at her campus, she became aware that the role of a principal was very complex and ever-demanding. Could an online program really prepare her for the real responsibilities of a principal's position?

When Amanda entered her first administrative position, she felt prepared. According to her credentials, she met all the requirements to serve as a school administrator at the high school level. Amanda was hired to serve as an assistant principal of curriculum and instruction in a 99% at-risk, urban high school.

The reality is that having the credentials to fill a position and being prepared to meet the demands and expectations of the position are two different things. She was thankful for the connections she had made in her online program with teachers who were similar to her in ambition and now were facing similar struggles as they all transitioned into leadership roles. This connection was critical to Amanda's success in navigating the changing roles she was experiencing.

Recent graduates had shared with Amanda's cohort that they too felt prepared for educational leadership. Specifically, these alumni expressed an appreciation for the online environment because of two primary aspects that contributed to their effectiveness as school leaders: written communication and mindfulness. One alumnus expressed that he discovered the power of thinking through his thoughts before responding to questions, dilemmas, and new ideas.

Prior to his experience in the online program he felt compelled, even pressured to engage immediately with a verbal response to the inquiries of others. Without the understanding of the power of reflective response, he would have made poor initial decisions only to later discover that he'd have had a much more effective solution if he had taken the time to craft his thoughts on paper.

Using mindfulness in communication seemed to be a logical practice of any school leader, but Amanda realized very quickly that she was able to read the ideas of others several times before she drew conclusions about how she actually felt about the scenarios.

In the quick-paced life of a school administrator, it is often tempting to just give an answer in the moment and hope it works out well. Now, she and other alumni had experienced the power and effectiveness of pausing to consider the viewpoints of others and then to contemplate mindfully what response is actually the best course of action.

After a month of adjustments and reflections, Amanda was in a groove. Often Amanda wondered to what degree her online principal preparation program contributed to her success. As she reflected on her experiences in the online program, she realized that her concerns about field experiences, types of assignments, and the development of personal dispositions were on target as very critical to her sense of preparedness. Each of these was delivered and completed in a way that clearly demonstrated for Amanda how to use these learning experiences in real-life scenarios.

TRANSFERABLE ONLINE EXPERIENCES

As a teacher, Amanda had worked diligently to create meaningful learning experiences for her students. She understood that instruction without meaning and purpose was ineffective. For this reason Amanda created projects that were aligned with the state standards, but that allowed students the freedom to guide their discoveries and to use concepts that they found meaningful.

As a social studies teacher, she allowed them to research different times in history from unique perspectives so they would find the research more interesting. Most valuable to Amanda was that the students developed a sense of ownership in their learning, and that success would guide their understandings of learning in the future. Amanda was looking for an online program that matched her teaching philosophy because she knew her experiences and assignments in this process would be significant in preparing her to be an effective principal.

The program that she chose incorporated a variety of methods for instruction, learning, and assessment. The differentiated approach to the assignments was fulfilling and allowed Amanda to direct her own learning according to her particular interests and perceived needs.

Specifically, Amanda found an online program that used a variety of assessment methods including a portfolio, team projects, and individual reflections. The reflective aspect of the coursework allowed her to discover how she would incorporate the new concepts and leadership strategies into her teaching philosophy. The assignments were a mix of individual research, team efforts, and discussions among her classmates that were often controversial and led to some rather heated threads in the discussion board.

Amanda realized immediately that the tone portrayed in a post can be misunderstood, so she carefully crafted her responses to keep the dialogue healthy and useful for guiding her understandings of how to respond, plan, and evaluate circumstances and programs in her new position.

This diligence paid off as Amanda was able to understand how to craft effective messages to her teachers, parents, and district employees. She also recognized that she had developed a strong work ethic because she was required to manage her time wisely to complete the projects with others as well as her individual assignments.

The time-management component was valuable because as a new administrator she was constantly trying to determine where to place her efforts and energy and at what point she needed to pass off responsibilities to others. The program design fostered these skills and abilities naturally because of the combination of independent and co-constructed learning that was embedded into the assignments and assessments.

FIELD EXPERIENCES

Field experience was a required component of Amanda's online program. A full semester of job shadowing was designed to give the future school leaders genuine experiences and opportunities to discover how the concepts and principles being learned in the classes synthesized into daily practices.

Amanda was somewhat nervous as she introduced herself to her new mentor, Mrs. Herrera. This powerful female principal had been selected after much consideration because she was leading an educational environment that was similar in nature to the type of school and student population that Amanda aspired to serve.

The matching process was a learning experience in itself because Amanda was required to interview five different principals at five different locations. The challenge was the expectation that Amanda would identify five school environments with principals that she felt were worthy of shadowing, and each had to meet the criteria that Amanda had developed in an earlier assignment that profiled the type of school environment she would seek as an ideal match for her passions and talents. The online program required all principal candidates to create their own professional field experiences.

Through that process, Amanda learned the value of asking the best questions and listening attentively to the answers, and how to ask the critical follow-up questions to gain insights and clarity. Another benefit was that Amanda had met five school leaders that served her desired demographic, which immediately opened the doors for future employment. Understanding how to identify the right "fit" for each principal candidate was an integral aspect of the design of the program that Amanda selected.

After a few weeks with Mrs. Herrera, Amanda realized that her online program was preparing her professionally. She found her assignments to be relevant and was able to contribute in significant ways to the decisions made by her mentor. It seemed that Amanda had made a good choice in selecting her online program.

Mrs. Herrera commented on several different occasions and shared with her field experience advisor that Amanda seemed aware and capable of identifying problems before they manifested into crisis situations. Also, her field experience advisor had been informed that Amanda's experiences with the district had brought to light the credibility of online programs.

TYPES OF ASSIGNMENTS

Technology was not Amanda's strong suit and she feared that she would not be able to navigate the complexities of the online learning environment. Would her lack of technology know-how prevent her from reaching her goal? At first, there were terms she did not understand, like "thread," "stream," and "post." These terms had completely different meanings for her and as she started to engage in the online process, she found herself spending more time on the phone with technical support than actually doing the work for her classes. Eventually, she got the hang of it and was able to shift her fears and frustrations toward the coursework.

Amanda realized that she was out of touch with technological advances, terms, phrases, and common practices of navigating social media and websites. The online program required her to become familiar with all the major social media exchanges, and to be comfortable navigating and using them for professional purposes.

She realized that being in the classroom for five years had taken a toll on her ability to connect with her students and their parents. This was a valuable insight and she appreciated recognizing the importance of social media for educational purposes.

Throughout the online program, Amanda found herself learning to produce videos and stream them, and how to create a YouTube account for her staff and students to access trainings and information easily. She also learned that this is an efficient tool for creating shared spaces for her staff to communicate about instructional practices.

Several of her assignments were able to be used in her portfolio to demonstrate her principal competencies. Ultimately, this was the beginning of a storehouse of trainings that she would rely upon to overcome the barriers of time and space with her staff.

The research requirements were directly related to areas that Amanda chose to focus on professionally. She underwent a personal analysis of her strengths and weaknesses regarding the principal competencies and used the findings to guide her assignments and projects. For example, her understanding of special education law was rated too low, so she chose to focus two of her video assignments on this topic. Her freedom to use the outcomes of her personal analysis was liberating because she knew every assignment was serving multiple purposes.

PERSONAL DISPOSITIONS

Teaching dispositions was not a new concept for Amanda. She knew in her heart that some teachers lacked certain understandings about diversity and student needs, but never was quite able to move beyond her own limited understandings of others. She actually thought she could do something "to" her students to improve their circumstances.

In the online program, Amanda quickly realized that the diversity of her cohort would provide a platform to increase her understanding of cultural differences. She was no longer limited to shared experiences with others from her same region, demographic, and cultural background.

Amanda thought she was familiar with how she could impact the lives of others, but quickly realized that she had some deep-seated beliefs and values that were prohibiting her from truly being effective as a teacher. In her mind, she thought creating mirrored lives for her students would solve their challenges. If they acted like she did, took the steps she took, and mirrored her behaviors and practices, they would find deliverance from their limited lives. She was ignorant and did not understand that she was imposing her own beliefs while undermining the value of her students' personal experiences and cultural understandings.

Amanda quickly learned that she had made wrong assumptions and had incorporated oppressive practices into her classroom processes. The online environment opened her eyes to the world of others and the value of differences. Freire (1998) explained,

> It is fundamental for us to know that without certain qualities or virtues, such as a generous loving heart, respect for others, tolerance, humility, a joyful disposition, love of life, openness to what is new, a disposition to welcome change, perseverance in the struggle, a refusal of determinism, a spirit of hope and openness to justice, progressive pedagogical practice is not possible. (p. 108)

The experiences with others gave immediate credence to this powerful statement. Amanda was in a state of personal growth and would use that journey to inform her educational leadership practices.

She was challenged to change and in the beginning she was reluctant to accept that she had been guilty of limiting the contributions of her students. As she prepared to incorporate these new understandings into her leadership practices, Amanda determined that she would no longer do things "to" or "for" others, but "with" them.

The online environment provided a space in which Amanda was assigned to work with others who challenged her beliefs and values. She determined that there was strength in working with others who were not perfectly aligned with her beliefs and attitudes, and that her core beliefs were valuable and reliable for guiding her decisions as an educational leader.

JOB SEARCH WITH AN ONLINE DEGREE

Amanda had been warned that online programs were not considered as credible as traditional face-to-face programs. This reality, if it were true, would potentially undermine her ability to be hired into the school and for the position of her choice. Amanda did not just want the first available position.

She desired a particular school setting and wanted to work with a leadership team that shared her passion for student success. What if those school environments were prejudiced against online programs? Would she find herself implicated in false understandings or limited by preconceived ideas regarding the online learning environment?

The field experience contributed to Amanda's confidence that she was indeed prepared for the responsibilities of leadership. Receiving affirmation from her mentor and from the various interviews she conducted prior to selecting her field experience contributed to a positive sense of self-efficacy. This in turn allowed Amanda to demonstrate her preparedness and abilities in the various job interviews.

She did not have difficulty obtaining interviews. Some hiring administrators were more skeptical than others, but she found herself explaining the value of her program experiences and how her experiences would synthesize into her leadership style. Ultimately, she received more than one offer and was able to move into an administrative role that she desired.

PREPAREDNESS TO FULFILL AN ADMINISTRATIVE POSITION

The test began—Was she prepared by the program she chose? Did she have the skills, talents, abilities, disposition, and knowledge to meet the demands and expectations of her new position? The answer was yes: she was as prepared as anyone could be for the challenges facing her as a new administrator in a high-need high school.

Ironically, another assistant principal was hired at the same time who had taken a different route for his certification. He had attended a traditional face-to-face program. Their personalities were completely different and their talents were unique, but both of them were prepared, as well prepared as could be expected for first-year administrators.

That brings up another question. Expected by whom? Was Amanda satisfied with her level of preparation for this position? Was her principal satisfied? These are the questions that are most important to consider for all programs. Are the candidates satisfied, and are the employers satisfied?

Amanda was satisfied because she knew that she applied herself to the online degree program and took every opportunity to maximize her learning. Amanda believed her performance reviews and the increasing responsibilities that were entrusted to her indicated that she had met her principal's expectations.

CONCLUSION

In retrospect, Amanda believes that she chose a quality online program that fostered growth and understanding, which was critical to her success as an educational leader. She was able to maintain her life responsibilities while progressing through the online program, despite a move across the country. The flexibility of the program allowed her to test in the state in which she lived, even though it was a different state than when she began the program.

If she had made the decision to pursue a traditional face-to-face program, she would have likely invested money and time only to have a few courses transfer into a new program in the new location. This decision was clearly the correct path for Amanda. Her success as an educational leader has affirmed that she does have the qualities, knowledge, and abilities to lead successfully.

KEY POINTS

- Online learning environments are not all created equal, so be sure to create specific questions as you select which is the best fit for you.
- Technology is not as scary as it seems and there will be support until you feel comfortable.
- Taking online courses keeps you current with technology trends and enhances your ability to integrate social media into your role as an administrator.
- If you are prepared for the work, have created relevant experiences, and can articulate that with confidence, you can overcome most preconceived ideas about online programs.
- Experience is the most important aspect of learning and having a chance to work with others from various geographic, social, and cultural backgrounds is a benefit of the online environment.

REFERENCES

Freire, P. (1998). *Pedagogy of freedom: Ethics, democracy, and civic courage.* Lanham, MD: Rowman & Littlefield.

8

EPROFESSOR@ONLINE.EDU

Barbara Qualls

eProfessors can do their job while enjoying morning coffee, watching the birds and squirrels from the porch. eProfessors can do it while sitting on an airplane or waiting in the dentist's office. Or they can spiff up in a professor outfit and go sit at a real desk in a real office in a real building at a real university—and do the same thing.

Online teaching is a liberating experience. In a few years, it will be very interesting to check the perspectives of those instructors who have *only* taught online and whose students have only learned online. For now, even though online education is no longer new, we purveyors of it are ourselves, for the most part, products of traditional delivery systems and are feeling our way into the cyber world of teaching and learning.

Most new adventures are mixtures of fear and anticipation, second thoughts and certainty, loss and gain, metaphoric tears and laughter. Online instructing is all those things. If an instructor has already experienced a successful career in traditional education, the idea of narrowing your world to a computer screen seems like an incalculable loss.

Likewise, no longer having a rapt audience, eye contact, inside jokes, or even a classroom can seem like a bleak future. The truth, though, is that the new world of online education has experiences and options that are incredibly satisfying—so long as the instructor defines teaching and learning in broad brushstrokes and releases the tempting idea of comparing online to traditional delivery systems.

There are infinite ways to sort the impressions, perspectives, and observations of online instructors. For the structure of this chapter, those aspects of online instructing that are completely positive and without a downside will be the first considered. It should be no surprise that such a group of topics will be somewhat truncated. The second category will include some of the areas of online instruction that have potential for either positive or negative outcomes. And last, those areas that present challenges and require attention will be considered, along with some of the ways that those challenges may be neutralized.

AREAS WHERE ONLINE EDUCATION IS COMPLETELY POSITIVE

Online education may be the great equalizer, the giver of diversity that has been sought in education since *Brown v. Board* in 1954. It is certainly the answer to nondiscrimination in selection for students because there is no visual component, unless it is purposefully built into the structure of the online class. Likewise absent are audio cues that might trigger discriminatory bias. Thus, both students and instructors enjoy a degree of personal freedom that comes with the specific type of anonymity that online communion affords.

Certainly the absence of bias in selection for admission to an online program is an advantage. A related area that is likely a positive one but perhaps less clearly evident is in the awarding of grades. Without the visual and audio cues that exist in traditional classroom encounters between students and professors, it is likely that online grades are awarded with a higher level of freedom from bias.

Discrimination on the basis of race, gender, age, religion, lifestyle choice, location and address, make and model (or existence) of vehicle, beauty, weight/height, dental condition—virtually *any* of the various means that humans might use to discriminate among each other—is made much more difficult in online education.

Students (or, for that matter, instructors) who face physical limitations may find online education a godsend. Mobility issues are dissolved. Assistive technological devices can minimize hearing and visual limitations. Many aspects of compliance with the Americans with Disabilities Act are much easier and virtually without cost in online instruction. A whole new world of educational opportunity may open for some students with disabilities.

Online education is convenient for both teachers and students. Louis J. Camuti, D.V.M., led the unlikely career of feline-only veterinarian in New York City who only treated patients through house calls. He did this because cats, being the high-strung creatures they are, were unduly stressed when transported through noisy and frightening NYC traffic and were unwelcome on the subway.

His career is archived in a series of stories in the autobiographical *All My Patients Are Under the Bed: Memoirs of a Cat Doctor.* In our own way, online professors make virtual house calls at all hours of the day and night, but we do so at least in part for the convenience of our own "patients"—maybe *All My Students Are Wearing Pajamas: Memoirs of an eProfessor.*

The convenience of anywhere, anytime for engaging in online coursework is an extremely seductive selling point for busy and committed students. It is equally seductive for professors who have varied interests or other need for unstructured time.

The allure of convenience is broader than in scheduling time for classwork, though. With online education, students and teachers can relocate, maintain multiple residences, and take advantage of travel opportunities—all without jeopardizing their instructional program or employment.

Online education is unquestionably more accessible than traditional brick-and-mortar classrooms for students. Presumably, more students are enrolled in college programs and are actively pursuing degrees and certification than would be the case without the availability of online education.

Easy math: If more students can access higher education through online coursework, more teachers for those students are needed. Thus, more teaching jobs. However, those jobs are frequently adjunct positions with swollen class loads, but that is another argument altogether. Students can access their course material anywhere and anytime. Likewise, the professor can also access the course to update it, evaluate student submissions, chat/advise/answer questions for students—again, anywhere and anytime.

Just as the student can hold down a full-time job, raise a family, or do any other of life's activities without postponing higher education, so the professor can also pursue other activities both professional and personal, without the burden of regimented class meeting times or office hours.

Perhaps one of the most beneficial of the purely positive components of online education is that it forces the release of the guru-guree model. Physical presence with intentional or unintentional intimidation as well as social shaming all contribute to the dynamic in traditional face-to-face classrooms. All that is gone in online education. Some new or reluctant online instructors may fear the loss of control that online education represents.

In fact, when online or distance education was first introduced, one recurring teacher fear was that it was a precursor of automated instruction that would make traditional teachers obsolete. However, teachers who rest their effectiveness in their capacity for in-person intimidation will likely fail, whether online or in a traditional setting.

For some time, education at all levels has been undergoing a metamorphosis that redefines traditional roles for students as well as for teachers. Hands-on, learner-centered, constructivist—by whatever name, the teaching and learning continuum has been in flux for the last several decades.

A rhyming descriptive phrase applied to the process of transforming the continuum has been adopted by many theorists, as well as serving as a marketing strategy for Apple computers: teachers are becoming less a sage on the stage and more a guide on the side. John Watson (2014) has made a convincing argument for seeking new terminology for that instructional reformation, suggesting that "guide on the side" implies a lower, less important role for teachers.

The role of the teacher in online education is a serious one. While it may not look like traditional teaching, the responsibility of the online educator is precisely the same as that of the traditional teacher, but the ways that responsibility is executed are more varied, more flexible, often more content-directed, and, in some cases, just more. Online education is not teacherless. Just guruless.

AREAS WHERE THERE IS POTENTIAL FOR EITHER POSITIVE OR NEGATIVE OUTCOMES

Online education stops the nonsense of teacher as "performance artist"—those characters who inspired the phrase "Those who can, do. Those who can't, teach." It also stops the anecdotal old codger strolling around telling tales of "When I was in the classroom . . ." while jingling keys and coins (or worse) in his pockets.

A captive audience, one that is by definition in a subservient position, is exactly what a performance artist masquerading as a teacher needs. Happily, online instruction puts that out of business. At the same time that the abuses of the performance artist are curtailed, though, the genuine voice of experience is also muted in online education.

Presumably, the professor has at his disposal observational asides, personal and professional experiences, deeper and more detailed knowledge than the course content provides. In online instruction, the professor is not allowed the questionable luxury of depending on war stories to fill up class hours, but at the same time, students do not have easy access to the benefits that could be afforded by an experienced voice.

One would think that being a technophile would be a good thing for an online professor. That, however, is not universally the case. Since students are using a wide array of receptor machines including home laptops, desk PCs, and university systems, the quality of their reception varies greatly. Many will not have easy access to high-enough-speed Internet, while others may have bandwidth limitations. Virtually all of them will access course material from several different devices.

For all those reasons, the possible glitches related to application issues, transfer platforms' incompatibility, subscription variations, software edition variations, dead links, and a host of other barrier possibilities are endless. Most students and professors will also use mobile devices for at least a portion of their course-related activity.

Some eProfessors just like new gadgetry and are deeply into the bells/whistles syndrome. A personal experience occurred with the realization that students were not nearly as entertained by a jumping textbook animation as was hoped. An admission had to be made that the amateur use of splashy visual and sound effects was the 2015 version of

the creepy professor who uses knock-knock jokes to "break the ice"—
but succeeds only in adding another frosty layer.

In addition to their highly questionable utility, tech tricks need to be
evaluated by online professors to consider the proportional amount of
time such toys devour, the amount of bandwidth and download time
they cost students, and—most of all—whether the professor's time
could be more constructively used in improving the course.

Everson (2009) also has pointed out that embedding extra technology into online courses has the added risk of becoming obsolete too soon
to make the time investment worthwhile. No emoji for a raised eyebrow
is as effective as the real-deal deadpan look that silently says, "Surely
you didn't really mean to say that." Even though LOL, :-) and other
social media shorthand is native for many and natural for most, it does
not come close to a warm laugh or patted hand.

Now, all that said, there are many passionate devotees to all that is
new, all that is techno-cool, and they will not sway from their position
that a primary function of an online professor is the use of an array of
technical applications. They, however, are incorrect in holding that position. LOL.

Time is a deceptive concept when considered in the context of online education. The positive side of time is that there is a lot of it, there
are few predetermined constraints on it, and the online instructor has
wide latitude in how to use it. Concepts, instructions, and acknowledg-
ments that can be achieved in seconds in traditional classes require
maybe hours of teacher time in online courses in preparation of detailed explanation, back story, timelines, format instruction, conse-
quences, and assessment rubrics.

Introductory courses in an academic discipline require a larger
amount of instruction preparation time because new terminology, phil-
osophic foundations, and historical perspective all must be established
without an existing framework of knowledge. For example, courses that
fall early in a degree plan require the introduction of a number of new
ideas and new language, but also new ways of considering philosophy
and sense of identity.

A more specific example of that identity shift might be a degree and
certification program that helps classroom teachers make the mental,
emotional, and professional shift to the role of educational leader, preparing for the roles of principal and other supervisory positions, such as

an M.Ed. program with concomitant administrator certification. Achieving that identification shift is hard for students and perhaps the online environment makes that transition even more difficult.

Another type of introductory course can also be a time drain. That is the set of courses that are first encountered by the online student. A whole adventure of learning passwords, log-on steps, how to navigate within instructional management systems, new technical terminology, how to determine Internet connectivity, where/how to submit assignments, and how to utilize help and assistance modules all await the new online student.

Even though the actual responsibility for instruction in all those areas may belong to someone other than the online professor, it is the online professor who will be the singular surefire responder on the receiving end of a desperate midnight email inquiry from students new to online education. Many repetitive emails and text messages can be avoided by spending time at the beginning with complete and detailed step-by-step instructions.

A final area with both positive and negative potential involves student participation. At first consideration, it would seem that online participation would be inferior to the freewheeling discussion that can occur in traditional classrooms. Closer examination, though, may deflate that concept. Discussion boards are common strategies in many online classes and can take on a number of different formats.

The most common strategy is to request individual responses to a stated idea/concept/scenario, then ask students to return to the board and respond to a specified number of other students' comments. In this manner, it is almost guaranteed that all students will participate. In a traditional classroom, it is likely that a few students will dominate discussion and that others will not engage at all. It is possible (likely) that some traditional students are not even active listeners.

The online discussion board levels that playing field—at least in part. There is a significant difference in the nature of student participation in online discussion, though. Because there is time to consider and organize thoughts, select words, and "take back" unintended statements, the initial contributions are probably better than they might be in a live class.

However, the immediacy of response feedback and reaction that is exhilarating in a live class is absent in online discussion. So, while the quality of contribution may be better, creativity and scaffolding with other students' ideas may be less satisfying than in traditional discussion.

Experienced traditional classroom teachers may dislike the regimentation of grading and assessing that is necessary for online instruction. Although consideration is given to student motivation in the final part of this chapter, online students probably need a specific point value assigned to each portion of their discussion board activity in order to ensure that it takes place. Another aspect of online discussion that differs dramatically from traditional live classes is that it takes much more time online. Everson (2009) suggests combining topics and allowing at least a week for responses.

AREAS THAT PRESENT CHALLENGES IN ONLINE INSTRUCTION

Few educators would even try to argue that building relationships with students is not a vital part of the teaching and learning continuum. However, the very nature of an online relationship is considerably different from the same process in a traditional classroom.

Accepting and embracing the new role is not easy for teachers accustomed to face-to-face communication.

No matter how skillful or frequent e-communication between teacher and student may be, it is still less personal than face-to-face talk. One by-product of that depersonalization is that online students tend to be more confrontational and less deferential with their side of the online relationship.

This new and more nearly equal role is not always welcomed by the teacher. When the relationship survives those early collisions, though, the result is well worth the effort. Who is in a better position to offer honest suggestions for improvement of instructional strategy than the actual client? When a car manufacturer wants to improve his product, he asks car buyers what they need and want. Online instructors should do the same.

In fact, most online programs have an embedded component for student evaluation and assessment and results are carefully examined and utilized. That exposure to criticism from students is a relatively new experience for many online instructors, though, and one that is sometimes uncomfortable.

Learning from students, whether how to improve course content or delivery or to accept aggressive challenge to content positions, involves learning to embrace a new role for traditional teachers. Nolen (1994) posited an involved explanation of why teachers find it difficult to accept "instruction" from students:

> If one admits that students can contribute to decisions about their schooling, that they have something to offer us, this distance (between students and their teachers and administrators) is eroded. And with distance lies safety, insulation from students' potentially difficult and disturbing lives. Hierarchies are maintained. If we don't listen to our students' critiques, we don't have to learn the shortcomings in our own teaching. We don't have to publicly address the powerlessness we may feel in the face of a difficult teaching situation. We don't have to explore the limits of our knowledge of the subjects we teach, or the places where those subjects intersect with our students' lived experiences. So we maintain the silence, the expectation that the teacher will make educational decisions, and the students should bow to their superior knowledge of subject matter and curriculum. (p. 32)

Although Nolen's (1994) remarks were not specifically geared to online education, they are certainly applicable. A teacher or student who is made uncomfortable by aloneness will face extra challenge in an online environment.

As was discussed as a two-sided observation, the workload for online instruction has a nonnegotiable component that some may find onerous. Because the format of online courses requires a great deal of printed detail and instruction, the creative engagement of the instructor is seriously frontloaded.

That, of course, means that an online instructor has to be a self-starter, practice self-discipline, adhere to deadlines, and work within templates established by software systems, as well as comply with all aspects of institutional requirements for course and syllabus construction. Some instructors may appreciate the defining structure, but more will probably find all that "help" a tight fit.

In further examination of the relationship between online students and teachers, it must be recognized that motivation of students is harder. All the visual, expressive, aural cues of traditional classrooms are absent and are not replaced with other more positive motivational tools. Most instructors find it simplest to reduce most interchanges to point values and limit optional "do it because it is a good idea" assignments (Everson, 2009).

In the best situations, that mechanical give/take grows into a more genuine instructional sharing. When that better relationship does not develop, at least the content is sent and delivered, assimilated and evaluated. Motivation of online students remains an area of challenge and one that will benefit from thoughtful research and experimentation.

The most tangible exhibition of the online student/teacher relationship is the email exchange. Although most 21st-century educators are comfortable with the use of email, ease, frequency, and depth of use all vary. In a traditional class, a set of instructions can be shared verbally one time, questions entertained with students listening and learning from each response. The same exercise in online instruction may generate many more questions, each one presented as if it were a totally new and original thought.

For that reason, an online instructor's patience and tolerance for repetition can be tested. He does learn, though, that clear, unambiguous instructions, posted in precisely the same way in several places, will pay high dividends in decreasing repetitive questions. When those repetitive questions and pleas for clarification come, it is best to accept them as learning experiences: remember that the question is *not* repetitive for the individual student and that the next set of instructions should be more detailed.

As difficult as student motivation is, teacher motivation is even more complex. Building collegial relationships must be intentional. In a traditional environment, physical geographic space is shared for several hours every day, equipment and supplies are easily shared, even lunch and coffee time are shared. Online instructors have few of those sharing opportunities as naturally occurring events.

The result is that online instructors may retreat into silo-like professional lives and experience collegial relationships primarily through the same online presence that defines their teaching. Some may find that situation exactly to their liking, but many others may find it constricting and unsatisfactory.

While online education is a field ripe for research of best practices, it is currently not without some foundational study. Over a decade ago, Smith, Ferguson, and Caris established some points of comparison between online and traditional instruction (2001). In the intervening years, much improvement in online instruction has taken place.

In fact, it is likely that online education has evolved into a discipline in its own right and no longer needs to be defined in terms of how it differs from traditional instruction. However, many of today's online instructors still are immigrants from traditional classrooms or were traditional students themselves so that the comparison is still instructive.

As has been observed, the level of written detail, specificity of instructions, and regimentation of instructor expectations are much more crucial for online instruction. Many college professors find production of that level of clerical detail a tedious task. It just cannot be assumed that "they should already know that"—the communication medium for online instructor/student is different from verbal.

The nuance and richness of verbal communication is missing and a wise instructor will *not* assume that lectures, examples, activities, or assignments that work well in traditional settings can simply be transferred to slides for an online presentation (Smith, Ferguson, & Caris, 2001).

SUM TOTAL: POSITIVE, NEUTRAL, CHALLENGES

In many respects, online education remains uncharted territory. Leaders and standards are emerging. That is exciting and cause for a celebration of freedom, but also included in that paradigm is the need to fight the vague but persistent perception of online education being a second-rate product. There are far too many people who still remember the "talking heads" of early distance learning.

At one point in the not-too-distant past, "correspondence courses" were used only for what were considered "blow off" courses to be knocked out during the summer in order to open up room in the long-term schedule for "real" courses. Even more telling were those correspondence or online courses that were taken to compensate for a failed course in "real" education.

In a very short time, though, that reality has changed so that viable K–12 programs, a bevy of instructional and licensure programs, and whole degree and certification programs are now commonplace. They exist both as startup programs built expressly for online delivery and as products of established traditional schools, colleges, and universities.

The role and responsibility of the online educator are just as important as those of a traditional teacher. In fact, they are the *same* as those of a traditional teacher. Marginalization only happens when an educator abdicates his or her role. What the execution of that role looks like is different between traditional and online instructors.

However, the emergence of instructional reform that focuses on student performance and student achievement and far less on teacher performance means that teachers are changing in both the traditional and online arenas. Examination of a list of dispositions desired in online instructors is instructive. There are no characteristics that define the National Education Association's online instructor that are not also highly desirable traits for any teacher in any environment:

Online instructors

- are prepared well to use modern information, communication, and learning tools
- are motivated self-starters who work well without constant supervision
- are student-centered and flexible, while maintaining high standards
- are able to promote online dialogue to deepen the learning experience
- are able to collaborate with students and student support staff/ systems to further student participation and success in the online course
- specify learning objectives, and design activities and authentic assessments to measure mastery of the stated objectives
- are able to use adaptive technologies to meet individual student needs
- possess a sense of humor and are able to "project" their personality through developing an "online voice"

- exhibit mastery of the online environment(s) and the learning/content management system(s) to be used
- are effective in written communications
- have completed professional development specifically geared to teaching online (National Education Association, n.d., pp. 13–14)

Being an online professor is probably a different experience for a traditionally educated transplant than it will be in the very near future when an online professor may well be an online product, too. For now, a clear and solid knowledge of academic content remains the common element spanning both traditional and online education that is the first necessity for success in either environment. As online education ages and matures, perhaps the primary drawbacks of relationship building and transfer of professorial experience can be mitigated.

CONCLUSION

There are distinct positive aspects that make online higher education more highly desirable than the traditional brick-and-mortar model. These include a much easier path to achieving diversity among both students and faculty, easier and less expensive accommodation for students with physical limitations, convenience for all users, accessibility to higher education for a broader clientele (and increasing robustness in the business of higher education), the decline of the teacher-centered educational model, and open field experience for student-centered education.

Although the positive and productive aspects are convincing, there is an equally strong series of online higher education characteristics that have capacity for success or its absence. They include the demise of the teacher-as-performance-artist. While online teachers cannot ramble, tell endless stories, or otherwise ad lib their way through classes, they also have a much more difficult task in sharing viable experiential knowledge.

The temptation to use and overuse technology, which may become obsolete before its cost-effectiveness has been realized, is a serious threat. Some professors of online education find the skewed work distribution schedule a challenge.

For first-time student users, introductory online courses can some-times be as much about how to operate the instructional management system as they are about the course content. Online education does allow student-to-student discourse, but it is much more difficult and time-consuming than in traditional education.

The most troubling aspect of online education that is less effective than traditional models and for which no sufficient remedy has been found as of yet is the difficulty in building strong teacher/student rela-tionships and bonds.

Email as the primary communication link is adequate for sharing content knowledge and progress but is far more ponderous than the speech, facial expression, nuance, tone, and immediacy that are luxuries of traditional face-to-face classrooms. Motivation, both for the student and for the professor, is sometimes more difficult. For professors, the absence of easy and frequent collegial discourse is often a negative part of the online educational world.

KEY POINTS

Positive aspects of online instruction:

- Guaranteed improvement in diversity increases scope of higher education mission.
- Decline in bias in student selection improves richness and quality of student population.
- Improved equity and access for students with physical limitations at low/no cost raises compliance and opportunity.
- Convenience for both students and instructors may increase de-gree completion.
- Improved access to higher education for many students improves the workforce product and informed citizenry.
- Increase in the employment opportunities for instructors comes as a result of more students gaining access.
- Transformation of teacher/student role and relationship creates new teaching and learning paradigms.

Positive/negative aspects of online instruction:

- Decline of "performance artist" causes equal decline of the voice of experience.
- Focus on technology breakthroughs risks the loss of original content focus.
- Increase in time flexibility creates an increase in need for time management.
- Guarantee of total student participation also includes loss of spontaneity, immediacy, and group dynamics.

Negative aspects of online instruction:

- Shifting teacher/student power paradigm requires tolerance.
- Learning from students is sometimes uncomfortable.
- Workload for instructor is not evenly distributed across semesters/terms.
- University online systems and requirements may constrain academic creativity.
- Motivation of students, especially in abstract thought, is difficult.
- Communication is reduced to writing or telephone, loses some aspects of personalization.
- Teacher motivation and development of collegial relationships requires effort.
- Online instruction is evolving and still bears some residual stigma from early prototypes.

REFERENCES

Everson, M. (2009). 10 things I've learned about teaching online. *eLearn Magazine: Where Thought and Practice Meet.* Retrieved from http://elearnmag.acm.org/featured.cfm?aid=1609990.

National Education Association. (n.d.). *Guide to teaching online courses.* Retrieved from http://www.nea.org/technology/images/onlineteachguide.pdf.

Nolen, S. B. (1994). *What can we learn from students?* Paper presented at the annual meeting of the American Educational Research Association, New Orleans, LA.

Smith, G., Ferguson, D., & Caris, A. (2001, April 1). Teaching college courses online vs. face-to-face. *THE Journal.* Retrieved from http://thejournal.com/Articles/2001/04/01/Teaching-College-Courses-Online-vs-FacetoFace.aspx?Page=1.

Watson, J. (2014). Time to retire the phrase "guide on the side" [Web log post]. Retrieved from http://www.kpk12.com/blog/2014/05/time-to-retire-the-phrase-%E2%80%9Cguide-on-the-side%E2%80%9D/#comments.

9

ONLINE EDUCATOR PREPARATION PROGRAMS

Perceptions of the Gatekeepers

Ronny Knox and Michael Martin

Any discussion of online teacher preparation programs would be incomplete if we did not consider the viewpoints of principals and human resources (HR) directors. Columbaro and Monaghan (2009) refer to these two groups as gatekeepers.

Columbaro and Monaghan stress the importance of these gatekeepers when they state, "The economic climate causes students to place a high premium on whether online degrees translate into jobs and careers. This translation is dependent on the current hiring practices that are influenced by the organization's hiring gatekeeper's view" (2009, p. 1).

Getting that first job for the aspiring teacher really is predicated on the acceptance of online programs by these gatekeepers. Many of today's practicing principals and HR directors did not have the opportunity to experience online education as they were pursuing their undergraduate and graduate degrees, so it's only natural for them to gravitate toward the traditional face-to-face model as their preference for those they employ.

According to Huss (2007), times may be changing. Huss states, "The existing literature about employer attitudes toward online degrees is sparse, yet suggests that overall acceptance of distance learning is on the rise despite a stated preference for traditional degrees" (2007, p. 24).

The influence of the principal to allow a shift in hiring considerations is the first step to the acceptance of this route of educator preparation. In the majority of school districts across the nation, the hiring of campus staff rests with the campus principal and his or her team. Hiring recommendations are made to the superintendent for new campus staff based on the influence and recommendation of the principal.

For online programs to achieve employability goals for their students, they must persuade principals that there is no difference between the quality of training received by the teachers who have earned their degrees through an online program and those who followed the traditional face-to-face route.

Huss (2007) supports this belief when he states:

> If principals who recommend new teachers for classroom positions are receptive to the online degree and view it no differently than a traditional degree, a definite selling point for online education has been established . . . if these same principals express tentativeness about hiring online graduates for the classroom, a baseline for instigating dialogue between the e-learning community and administrators must be established to perhaps alleviate and overcome any undesirable perceptions. (p. 24)

This trust of the online program will come as more and more principals experience these new teachers on their campuses. These experiences will create questions for the gatekeepers to ponder as they travel down this path.

These questions to ponder cover both tangible and intangible topics, such as institutional concerns, acceptance by peers, perceived motivations, and ability to evaluate educator dispositions. All must be addressed with transparency and evaluative data to give online educator preparation candidates an equal opportunity to be considered as viable replacements for current staff openings. Preconceived prejudices of online versus traditional programs must be addressed in order for the discussion to move forward.

When exploring topics such as concerns or acceptance by peers regarding online teacher preparation programs and those who graduate from them, Columbaro and Monaghan (2009) cite the following reasons that an employer may feel hesitant about hiring someone with an online degree:

- lack of rigor,
- lack of face-to-face interactions,
- increased potential for academic dishonesty,
- association with diploma mills,
- concerns about online students' true commitment evident from regularly venturing to a college or university physical location, considered by some to be an important part of the educational experience. (p. 5)

These concerns are met with just as many positive influencing factors for a principal to hire a teaching candidate who matriculated through an online program. Columbaro and Monaghan (2009) posit the following influential factors:

- name recognitions/reputation of the degree-granting institution,
- appropriate level and type of accreditation,
- perception that online graduates were required to be more self-directed and disciplined,
- candidates' relevant work experiences,
- whether the online graduates were being considered for promotion within an organization or if they were vying for new positions elsewhere or in a new field. (p. 5)

The gatekeepers for a school district must consider all of these influences, positive and negative, when addressing the teaching and administrative needs they must fill. As many universities look to expand their market to reach a more diverse population, online programs are becoming more of the norm than the exception.

According to Allen and Seaman (2005) in their report *Growing by Degrees: Online Education in the United States*, "forty-four percent of all schools offering face-to-face Master's degree programs also offer them online" (p. 1). This number is only increasing; as Bob Barrett (2010) notes, "many virtual schools show annual growth rates between 20 and 45%" (p. 18).

Intangible influences also come into play when discussing influential factors for the gatekeepers on watch over the district's positions. As mentioned before, these influences fall under the categories of perceived motivations and teacher and administrator dispositions.

Motivations for choosing an online program can only be answered by the candidate. Was it a logistics issue over a more traditional program? Was it, as some principals may perceive, a "quick and easy" route to certification? Only the candidate knows the real answer and the candidate's ability to expound on these reasons may be the telling difference in an interview.

Teacher dispositions are even more intangible and subjective in an interview. Many believe the disposition of a teacher can really only be assessed in the classroom (see chapter 5) and to make judgments in an interview on this topic is certainly premature. Huss (2007) illustrates this point when he states:

> When discussing attributes like composure, empathy, enthusiasm, eye contact, fairness, humor, and initiative, the principals continually restated their beliefs that teacher affect needs to be witnessed by those who interact regularly with these individuals in classroom or laboratory settings. (p. 27)

It's important to note, too, that although student teaching and student internships do expose teaching candidates to real experiences in the classroom, there are times when successful student teaching experiences do not translate into successful teaching careers.

PRINCIPAL PERSPECTIVE

To really gain the proper perspective of the influence online programs have in the hiring practices and evaluative programs of campuses, we must go to the most prominent influencer, the principal. The authors interviewed principals from differing campus levels (elementary, middle school, and high school) to build the groundwork for this perspective.

The interviews included questions that delved into interview practices, observations in the classroom, and, finally, personal experiences with online programs. The answers were very candid and differed greatly based on the amount of experience the principal had in his or her career as a principal.

In regard to the questions that pertained to interviewing practices, the authors presented probes that asked the principals to posit on the following: (1) How much weight do you afford the type of education preparation program the candidate experienced, online or traditional? and (2) Which type of program would you prefer that your candidates complete? As stated before, the answers differed depending on experience level and campus level of the principal.

In initial job interviews, the majority of the principals admitted to asking candidates to describe their undergraduate program, and significant weight was placed on the quality and type of program. Below are excerpts from principals at different campus levels:

> *I asked them to tell me about their educational experiences and how they came to the teaching field. They will usually explain without me asking and this gives me an opportunity to judge the experience for myself.*—Elementary School Principal

> *Yes, I always ask their certification path and where they went to school. I like to find teachers who went the traditional route, but I find we are getting more and more applicants who took the alternative route.*—Middle School Principal

After reading this last principal's response, one important note needs to be made: in talks with the principals, and as the middle school principal's quote above demonstrates, they seem often to conflate "online preparation" and "alternative certification." These do not represent the same things, and full definitions of each term are provided in the next section of this chapter. For now, though, it's important to know that "online" refers simply to how a training program is delivered. Alternative certification represents a different training program entirely, with different curriculum, different requirements, and different expectations. The confusion between these two probably indicates that online programs have more work to do in the area of public relations.

The principals interviewed had more definitive opinions regarding their preference of the type of program they would like to see their candidates complete, though again, through their comments, they demonstrate conflation of traditional certification (which may or may not be online) and alternative certification (which likewise may or may not be online):

> *First of all I think it depends on their life experiences. However, I would prefer candidates that are younger to have gone through the university student teaching program.*—Elementary Principal

> *I prefer the traditional route. Alternative certification teachers still do not have the base of knowledge, the understanding of educational language, nor the classroom management skills that traditional candidates possess.*—Middle School Principal

> *I would prefer that the applicant graduated through a traditional program. My personal opinion is that it would have a significant impact on hiring an applicant. If two applicants applied for the same position, one was online, the other traditional, and both interviews were equal as far as quality, then the fact that one was a traditional teacher certification would tip the scale in their favor.*—High School Principal

The principals were also asked to share their perceptions in regard to strengths and weaknesses they observed from those candidates that had participated exclusively in an online program. In reviewing the responses, it's obvious that the principals continue to use "online" and "alternative" interchangeably.

Parsing the responses in an effort to separate the "online" comments from the "alternative" comments revealed a few common themes related to online education. Through their responses, the principals related a number of potentially significant strengths and weaknesses that must be considered in the hiring process.

Potential benefits:

1. Convenience and flexibility.
2. Expansion of opportunities to more students.
3. Affordability.

Potential drawbacks:

1. Lack of interactions in the classroom.
2. Lack of consistent follow-up.
3. Lack of collaboration.

Only one of the principals surveyed had actually participated in an online course. This principal is in the process of obtaining his master's online through a local university. His perception of an exclusive online program is as follows:

> I am currently enrolled in [online] educational leadership courses. My experience so far has been a positive one. The coursework is not overwhelming but does require some time to produce quality work. I have had the opportunity to meet a couple of my professors and have conversations with them. Although I do enjoy the ability to work at my convenience, I am the type of person that would benefit more from the traditional classroom approach. But, if that were the case, I'm not sure I would have pursued the certification if I had to attend classes at night. This sounds like I'm contradicting myself, that I prefer online but wish for traditional classroom setting.—High School Principal

Overall, while they delineate both potential benefits and potential drawbacks, the principals interviewed for this chapter express some ambivalence toward online learning. As noted earlier, this ambivalence is likely due to inexperience with the format. Online programs and candidates who were trained online must work diligently to overcome any ambivalence they face in the job market.

HUMAN RESOURCES PERSPECTIVE

The HR director of an organization, often referred to as the gatekeeper, often reviews applicant credentials more closely than do the principal and his or her committee. The HR director has a working knowledge of traditional versus online certification programs and the positives and potential negatives of each. This working knowledge is based on the HR director's thorough understanding of a few definitions.

Before an educator or committee member can really understand and participate in the application process, he or she must have an understanding of some basic educator definitions. As demonstrated by the ambiguity related to online and alternative forms of certification in the principal interview responses, it is imperative that everyone involved in the interview process understand these definitions. While the following list is not an exhaustive one, it provides administrators and committee members with a general understanding of some key terms.

Educator Preparation Program

An educator preparation program (EPP) is a state-approved course of study, the completion of which signifies that an enrollee has met all the state's educational or training requirements for initial certification or licensure to teach in the state's elementary or secondary schools.

A teacher preparation program may be a regular program or an alternative route to certification, as defined by the state. Moreover, the regular or alternative route to teacher certification can be found in all delivery methods, both online and face-to-face.

Traditional Program

The traditional program is one that requires students to attend classes face-to-face on a university campus. Students complete their certification requirements as part of their degree program. Field experiences, internships, and student teaching are critical components of this program.

Online Program

An online program is a program that requires all (or most) coursework to be completed online rather than attending courses on an actual university campus, though the curriculum and requirements are the same as those in the traditional university program. Students also complete their certification as part of their degree program, and field experiences, internships, and student teaching are also critical components of this program.

Alternative Certification

An alternative certification is a process by which a person is awarded a teaching license even though that person has not completed a traditional teacher certification program. In the United States, traditional teacher certification is earned through completing a bachelor's or master's degree in education, taking standardized tests (usually a Praxis test), and fulfilling additional state requirements.

Alternatively certified teachers typically possess a "non-education" bachelor's degree from an accredited college or university and are completing (or have completed) an alternative certification program while teaching full-time. Many alternative certification programs are not completed online. Field experiences, internships, and student teaching are *not* critical components of this program, as the candidate is usually teaching concurrently with the program.

Highly Qualified

Section 1119 of the No Child Left Behind Act (NCLB) of 2001 focuses on improving teacher quality at the local level. To achieve this goal, the act requires all teachers teaching core academic subject areas to meet specific competency and educational requirements. Teachers who meet these requirements are considered "highly qualified."

SCREENING CRITERIA AND QUALIFICATIONS

Once all members of the committee have a general understanding of the terms above and the application process, the screening of applicants begins. Of course, regardless of the applicant, an HR director must uphold the law and provide equal rights to all candidates throughout the entire process.

Principals and human resources managers are looking for certain "research-based, best practice" characteristics from potential applicants in addition to the "highly qualified" status. Applicants must be well versed in the content area for which they have applied.

The applicant must also have the proper credentials in order to be considered "highly qualified" as defined by NCLB. In most cases, the

HR director will review the applicant's college transcript looking at classes that correlate to the subject matter that will be taught. During this review, the HR director considers the major and minor undergraduate courses of study.

In a perfect world, HR directors would have an extensive pool of highly qualified applicants for all content areas. However, the reality of the matter is that certain areas such as math, science, special education, and bilingual education pose a staffing problem due to the lack of highly qualified applicants.

When finding a highly qualified teacher becomes an issue, the human resources manager may turn to those with alternative certification, which contributes in part to the prominence of alternative certification in the principals' interview responses above.

The National Education Association (NEA) found that alternative certification helps to recruit for content areas that are in high demand or hard to fill. The NEA also recognized that alternative certification programs can give large cities and rural areas a larger applicant pool to assist with filling the more difficult positions in a timely manner (Zumwalt & Craig, 2005). Oftentimes, the varied educator preparation programs allow HR directors some relief in hiring teachers in those "hard to fill" subject areas. However, the relief also creates a few concerns.

Lack of Training

HR directors have many concerns to think about during the screening and interview process. For example, as noted earlier in the principal interviews, HR directors are also often troubled by applicants that have chosen the alternative certification route. The mind-set is that these applicants may not be prepared for classroom management issues and may not be as familiar with the content of the subject they wish to teach.

Conversely, traditional teacher certification programs, whether online or not, offer potential teachers preparation and training that will help them with classroom management techniques. Also, traditional programs require teachers to student teach in their content area to give them hands-on training for effective classroom management. However, it should be noted that just because a student has completed a traditional program as well as student teaching doesn't mean that he or she won't have issues with classroom management or the subject matter.

Alternative Certification

Alternative certification programs are becoming increasingly more acceptable to prospective employers. As noted in the definition, alternative certification programs can be either face-to-face, hybrid, or online.

However, one must remember, the students wanting to obtain their initial teaching certification through the alternative certification route have already earned a bachelor's degree in some field of study. Through alternative certification, almost all preparation and training occurs on the job.

School districts are facing areas of shortage and alternative programs assist them in meeting the needs of their students. As noted in the definition of terms, an alternative certification route allows applicants who have received a bachelor's degree from an accredited institution of higher education an opportunity to enter the teaching profession within the same school year.

The applicant applies to an approved educator preparation program; in the case of the trade and industrial education certificates, experience may be substituted for a bachelor's degree. The educator preparation program reviews the applicant's college transcripts for the highest number of credit hours completed in the desired teaching content area. Once this process has been completed, the EPP endorses the applicant with the State Board for Educator Certification (SBEC) to allow the applicant to take a content area Texas Examinations of Educator Standards (TExES) exam.

Upon submission of passing scores on comprehensive examinations prescribed by SBEC as specified in section 230.21 of this title (relating to educator assessment), the applicant is considered highly qualified and eligible for hire by a school district. Once the applicant is hired by a school district, he or she, with the endorsement of the educator preparation program, must apply for a probationary certificate with SBEC. The holder of a probationary certificate must be a participant in good standing in an internship supervised by an approved EPP (19 Tex. Admin. Code § 230.37(d), 2012).

SBEC will issue the probationary certificate, which will expire one year from the date it is issued. The applicant must complete the required coursework for the respective educator preparation program within one year and take and pass the Pedagogy and Professional Responsibilities exam. After completion of the above qualifications, the EPP will make a recommendation for certification.

All of this is mentioned as a concern because this is a lengthy process and the school district must hire the alternatively certified teacher before he or she has gained any real, practical experience. The student teaching as a learning phase is missing from the alternative certification route. Instead, it is more of a "learn on the job" approach.

While there are concerns about the alternative certification approach, HR directors admit that there are some fantastic teachers that have received their teaching certification through the alternative approach. One HR director was quoted as saying, "Districts must have a dynamic mentoring system in place for *all* teachers. If this happens, it should not matter if a teacher has received his or her teaching certification through an alternative certification program or a traditional face-to-face program."

Online Programs/Courses

Online programs and courses are completely different than alternative certification. As evidenced earlier in this chapter, many individuals, including educators, tend to confuse the two. While someone can obtain an alternative certification by taking online courses, there is much more to online programs and online coursework.

HR directors share some of the concerns raised by the principals interviewed and noted earlier in the chapter. For example, some HR directors tend to be concerned about prospective online teachers and administrators lacking in areas such as collaboration and hands-on experiences; however, these concerns are likely rooted in their own inexperience with this format.

While there are concerns about online programs among those hiring, the bottom line is that more often than not, one cannot distinguish online courses or programs from looking at an applicant's transcript. The only way one might know this information is if the applicant shares it through his or her cover letter or application.

However, as noted in chapter 2, there are a few colleges or online degrees that hold the "diploma mill" reputation. In these instances, the HR director immediately recognizes the educator preparation program. If there is ever any question, one could check the accrediting organizations of the university.

The concerns listed above are valid concerns. However, there are concerns with the traditional face-to-face programs as well. It is important that those involved with the screening process focus on the qualifications needed for each individual position and hire the "right" person with those qualifications rather than focusing on the medium of delivery.

THE INTERVIEW PROCESS

During the interview process, one must set the concerns aside and look for the most qualified individual. In most districts, applicants seeking a position within the organization must first submit an application through an online system. This system is constantly monitored by the HR director and principals.

After a thorough review of applicants, a series of face-to-face meetings is set up between the applicant, principal, and site-based committee followed by a meeting between the applicant and the HR director. Within each interview, the applicant is presented with a set of carefully designed questions generated to achieve responses regarding the applicant's knowledge and experiences related to the desired position.

Most often, it is during the interview that principals and HR directors tend to discern information regarding the applicant's educator preparation program. During this time, the candidate may be asked several probing questions to determine the quality of his or her EPP. For example, the candidate may be asked to discuss possible field experiences, course collaboration opportunities, and rigor of assignments.

After the candidate's responses to these questions, the committee members and human resources director can better determine the quality of the educator preparation program. Note that it is the quality of the preparation program that is significant, *not* the delivery method. After all, all educator preparation programs have the same set of state and national standards.

CONCLUSION

As any educator will tell you, the days when students sat in straight rows of desks are gone. This applies to classrooms in the PK–12 setting as well as university classrooms. Instead, employers are seeing candidates apply for jobs that have sat in a variety of classrooms.

These classrooms may vary from face-to-face to online and sometimes a combination of the two. Thus, it is understandable that employers would begin seeing a new type of candidate applying for job postings. It is crucial that those hiring understand that times have changed and they will continue to see more and more online graduates.

Of course, this changes the recruitment and hiring process for HR personnel. It is imperative that organizations search for the most qualified candidate that is the "right fit" for the job. Therefore, it is important that those hiring keep in mind the future of the educational classroom.

The virtual classroom is becoming more and more prevalent in all education settings. In fact, teachers hired may possibly be teaching in a virtual PK–12 classroom. Thus, for those hiring teachers or administrators, it is prudent to keep in mind that "online" does not carry a negative connotation. Instead, online courses have much to offer. However, as stated earlier, those hiring must be cautious of diploma mills.

Through the selection and interview process, the HR director can discern the necessary information to determine the quality of the candidate's educator preparation program. However, it is the responsibility of the HR director to create and implement different hiring practices that enable the committee to determine the quality of the educator preparation program regardless of the means of delivery.

In the principal interviews, only one principal had experienced online courses, while the others had no personal experience with a virtual classroom. However, all principals interviewed had a somewhat negative opinion of online programs, and in many cases appeared to confuse online programs with alternative certification programs.

Perhaps this negative connotation comes from veteran administrators that are unaware of the components of an online course. Once "newer" administrators who have online course experience are hired, it is possible that the administrative mind-set toward hiring online graduates will change. It is certainly easier to approve of something if you have personally experienced it. In the meantime, it is the responsibility of the HR director to ensure that the best candidate is hired for the open position regardless of anything else.

KEY POINTS

- Many individuals with hiring authority, whether justified or not, may be skeptical of online programs.
- There is a difference between alternative certification and online programs.
- More and more teacher and administrative applicants have taken some online courses.
- It is the responsibility of the human resources director to create and implement different hiring practices that enable the committee to determine the quality of the educator preparation program regardless of the means of delivery.
- Hire the most qualified candidate for the job.

REFERENCES

Allen, I. E., & Seaman, J. (2006, March). *Growing by degrees: Online education in the United States, 2005. Southern Edition.* Needham, MA: The Sloan Consortium. Retrieved from files.eric.ed.gov/fulltext/EDU530063.pdf.

Barrett, B. (2010). Virtual teaching and strategies: Transitioning from teaching traditional classes to online classes. *Contemporary Issues in Education Research* 3(12), 17–20.

Columbaro, N. L., & Monaghan, C. H. (2009, Spring). Employer perceptions of online degrees: A literature review. *Online Journal of Distance Learning Administration* 12(1).

Huss, J. (2007, March 26). Online learning and undergraduate teacher preparation: The attitudes of principals toward hiring online graduates. In R. Carlsen, K. McFerrin, J. Price, R. Weber & D. Willis (eds.), *Proceedings of Society for Information Technology & Teacher Education International Conference 2007* (pp. 361–367). Chesapeake, VA: Association for the Advancement of Computing in Education (AACE).

19 Tex. Admin. Code § 230.37(d). (2012). Retrieved from https://texreg.sos.state.tx.us/public/readtac$ext.TacPage?sl=R&app=9&p_dir=&p_rloc=&p_tloc=&p_ploc=&pg=1&p_tac=&ti=19&pt=7&ch=230&rl=37.

Zumwalt, K., & Craig, E. (2005). Teachers' characteristics: Research on the demographic profile. *Studying teacher education: The report of the AERA panel on research and teacher education* (pp. 111–156). Mahwah, NJ: Lawrence Erlbaum Associates, Inc.

Part IV

Relevance

10

POLICIES, PRACTICES, AND FINANCIAL IMPLICATIONS

Janet Tareilo

Policies and practices that influence the workings of an educational system are established to guide and direct the actions of the people involved, the program experience, and the continuation of quality results that ensure students receive the education they deserve.

Policies provide a framework in which practices can be developed, maintained, and assessed, all in accordance with the beliefs and vision of the organization. This rings true for all entities that educate children, from kindergarten to high school and even postsecondary colleges and universities.

Beyond the public primary and secondary school settings, colleges and universities are responsible for preparing graduates that are both knowledgeable and employable. The concept of a postsecondary education that accomplishes these goals is undergoing a metamorphosis that cannot be ignored. With vast advances in technology, the brick-and-mortar, on-the-ground style of obtaining a college degree is slowly going the way of the dodo bird. Extinction may be closer than colleges and universities imagine. And its name is online learning.

Regardless of the delivery method used in higher education, face-to-face or online, the fact remains that established policies guide the instructional processes and are present through professors' syllabi, college and university expectations for student behaviors, and accreditation measures that hold higher education institutions to state and federal standards.

DEFINING POLICIES

The terms "policy" and "practice" are continually and unfortunately used interchangeably. However, their meaning is not the same and actions associated with these two terms are very different.

In terms of educational entities, practices are simply the actions that take place as a result of an existing policy. For example, most colleges and universities require professors and instructors to write a syllabus for every course they teach. The syllabus actually serves as a would-be agreement between the professor, student, and university.

Within the context of the syllabus, a professor adds contact and course information, a calendar of due dates for specific assignments, and policies that govern the agreement made between the student and the university such as attendance, grading, and academic dishonesty.

When writing a syllabus, a professor must take into consideration the above policies and more. If in a syllabus a professor states that a student has only three days to complete a missed assignment but the university policy allows five days for the completion of an assignment, the professor is out of compliance with an existing policy. If a student wanted to file an appeal to have the additional days to complete an assignment, the appeal would be approved. In essence, the language used in the professor's syllabus is a practice that violates a policy.

The meaning of "policy" remains subjective and, at best, pertains to its use and content. Fowler (2004) recognizes that the differing definitions grow from "physical conflicts . . . the meaning of power and the proper role of the government" (p. 8).

Fowler settles on one definition that encompasses the meaning of policy and how it relates to institutions of higher learning: "Policy is the dynamic and value laden process through which a political system handles a public problem. It includes a government's expressed intentions of official enactments as well as its consistent patterns of activity and inactivity" (2004, p. 9). These assertions are correct in that colleges and universities are most definitely in control of how policies are defined as well as associated practices.

When Fowler (2004) mentions how policies assist in solving public problems this speaks directly to the way technology is rapidly moving through the realm of higher education in terms of online instruction. Price (2008) points out that "schools at all levels are racing towards [a] profound transformation in learning" (para. 4). With just these two assertions for consideration, defining policies as they relate to online education must align to those associated with on-the-ground learning and, quite possibly, face new definitions.

WORKING POLICIES

Educational policies at the college and university level are also governed by state and federal guidelines that impact accountability and accreditation measures. In general, policies require institutions of higher learning to complete internal and external audits to ensure that program offerings meet established standards. Any online program claiming to provide a quality education for its students cannot escape the requirements of being an accredited program (Burnsed, 2011).

For instance, in the state of Texas, the Texas Higher Education Coordinating Board (THECB) sets the framework of requirements for online programs. This entity is committed to providing "program integrity" (THECB, n.d.). The board's actions align with federal mandates from the U.S. Department of Education. As related to online instruction, the board is responsible for maintaining the quality of online programs across Texas as well as establishing the policies that govern a program's approval process, course approval process, and accountability and accreditation practices (THECB, n.d.).

Having an entity that serves as a "watchdog" to ensure course and program quality helps to cement the practices associated with offering online degrees. Many accrediting agencies, such as the THECB, review the success of any program in meeting expected standards through site visits, reported data, and the success of the program graduates.

With the rise of online programs and the consideration of their availability and flexibility for students and institutions, policies for meeting standards are not diminished. In fact, colleges and universities must not delineate from their responsibilities to provide a college degree regardless of the method of delivery.

Having knowledge about policies does not always equate to an understanding of how those policies work in a higher education setting. Policies at the college level also govern the areas of curriculum, student and professor relationships, course offerings, and financial concerns.

Policies are put into play to ensure the legality of instilled practices by both the university and the faculty. Whether a brick-and-mortar or an online venue, adherence to mandated policies for colleges and universities is not an option.

Discussion about how the policies work at a higher level is all well and good, but how does a policy actually work at the student and faculty levels?

Most colleges and universities have a policy regarding academic honesty. Academic honesty pertains to a student completing his or her own work, giving credit to other authors, and using other sources for referencing purposes. "Cheating" on an assignment or test is not a new concept for higher education. What is a new concept is how this is defined for online students.

In a face-to-face setting, an instructor can usually tell if a student is trying to cheat on an assignment or tests. Professors in this setting are more likely to be able to determine whether possible cheating is taking place simply by the inhabited space of a classroom. However, a professor who teaches an online course does not always have that guarantee.

While most policies for academic honesty are clear in their expectations, the same policies hold true for online courses. Where a professor in a regular face-to-face classroom might be able to ascertain different handwriting from assignment to assignment or even be able to see "cheat sheets" being used, professors in the online world may have to subscribe to a program such as Turnitin, which searches for incidents of plagiaristic writing.

Policies also exist regarding curriculum offerings. Before a course or program is offered through an online delivery method, a review and approval system must be in place. Many times a college or university has an internal audit system for this purpose. The focus of the review and approval practice is to ensure that online courses align with the completion of a degree and meet the standards established for accreditation (THECB, n.d.).

As per Watson (2008, para. 22), policies will have to be undertaken that formalize, as well as standardize, the subject matter and content found in the online classes. These enacted policies should be a reflection of the already mandated guidelines for the delivery of face-to-face programs or degrees offered at an institution of higher learning.

IMPLICATIONS FOR POLICIES

To discount the impact of an online education and the variables that must be considered for its continued presence in higher education is a futile train of thought. Online learning and its various modes of delivery are here to stay.

In many cases, online learning is less expensive, provides a greater range of flexibility for students, is readily available to anyone anywhere, and still results in the completion of a college degree (Burnsed, 2011). However, even though many colleges and universities are moving toward more online offerings of their courses, the move from a traditional brick-and-mortar setting to a virtual classroom environment is still in its infancy with relationships to policies that govern the realm of higher education.

There are considerations that must be taken into account when assessing the effectiveness and quality of an education that is received from an online source. An earned degree equates to approximately 120 hours of study in a particular field, required content expectations are met, and the graduate is employable in his or her chosen profession (Carey, 2015, paras. 7–8). Policies are the threads that ensure the above expectations are met according to university, state, and federal guidelines.

Henig and Hess (2010) propose that policies are the vehicles used to "create smooth transitions" (p. 60). Such transitions are needed as those seeking college degrees morph from a student walking on a campus to a full-time employee who goes to college after work while sitting at his or her kitchen table. What cannot be bargained for is the quality of the education being offered; hence the need for policies that help a student transition with the university as it moves toward becoming a school offering advanced technological learning.

Implications associated with policies related to an online education system are often based on existing policies. Colleges and universities are under continuous scrutiny from state and federal entities. Most programs follow prescribed standards that meet the expectations for graduation and future employment for program completers. Institutions of higher learning are often "visited" by accreditation teams and judged on the manner in which they met or did not meet the required standards.

With policies and practices in place to guide the accreditation process, colleges and universities can establish graduation plans, complete internal reviews of course content, and require that authentic assessments be in place to evaluate candidate competency. Policies also allow programs to make decisions regarding candidates who do not meet established standards.

For instance, many colleges and university programs for teacher education require a candidate to maintain a certain grade point average (GPA). A policy is established with this purpose. If a candidate fails to meet the required GPA, the program has the authority, through the policy, to withdraw that student from the program. This action is one way colleges and universities try to ensure the continued quality of a program.

Burnsed (2011) writes that "online education will disturb the placid waters of American higher education. If this happens there will be a ripple effect on the regulations, governance, and accreditation standards" (para. 1). The regulation and governance issues Burnsed mentions relate directly to the establishment of policies that govern the instructional delivery methods at institutions of higher education.

Face-to-face course offerings at a college or university have always been governed by policies. The onset of online learning may change the instructional modality but not the requirement of governance. Cook and Kubatzke (2007) comment on the fact that as the number of online programs increases, so will the issues associated with them, and that some regulatory system has to be in place to address the "review of courses and programs" (para. 4). Watson (2008) adds, "Each variable associated with online learning has implications for policy and practice" (para. 8).

FINANCIAL IMPLICATIONS

Here are two facts that need no supportive literature or research data: (1) a college education is more costly than ever before; and (2) many entry positions in certain job markets require a college degree. The two facts perpetuate the continued need for a degree past high school. However, in today's economic situation, the acquisition of that degree presents some would-be students with many difficulties, especially financial ones.

Farmer and Weber (2009) speak to the fact that a "market demand for online coursework is gradually changing the face of higher education" (p. 8). Many colleges and universities are foregoing "night" classes and replacing them with online courses.

Osika, Johnson, and Buteau (as cited in Tareilo, 2009) note that almost two-thirds of colleges and universities across the country offer online courses. While policies and practices govern these offerings, the element of cost-efficiency must also be a consideration.

Shifting the means of instructional delivery from a brick-and-mortar setting to an online venue creates financial concerns for an institution as well as a participating student. Paul (2013) draws attention to the fact that any reform such as this one taking place in higher education with the onset of online learning "involves a changing in funding [considerations]" (p. 124).

Changes in state and federal funding measures directly impact the day-to-day practices of colleges and universities regardless of the way education is delivered. Needed monetary assistance helps fund new building projects, facilitates new program areas, assists with facilities improvements, and determines faculty and staff salaries. And for students, receiving financial aid is directly impacted.

In 2006, Congress passed a law that ended the requirement that colleges offer 50% of their coursework through a face-to-face delivery method in order for students to receive financial aid (Romano, 2006). This meant that if a college or university wanted to increase its offerings of online programs its students would not be penalized from the standpoint of losing the ability to apply for and receive financial aid. Clearly, as Romano (2006) attests, moving from a brick-and-mortar setting to an online learning model is simply economically driven.

Where colleges and universities are concerned, the state and federal governments still have the right to regulate and distribute "their" money the way they see fit among the educational systems found on these campuses (Bidwell, 2014). Bidwell (2014) continues commenting on the financial responsibilities of colleges when mentioning that governing agencies that invest monetarily in the education of students expect those receiving a college degree to be employable.

Basically, if this goal is not achieved, institutions should expect the government agencies to want their money back. Even the U.S. secretary of education, Arne Duncan, stated, "Regulations [such as these] are necessary to ensure that colleges accepting federal funds protect their students, cut costs [where possible] and improve outcomes" (as cited in Bidwell, 2014, para. 3).

Regardless of the age, gender, financial status, or educational ability of a student, making the decision to seek and complete a college degree requires careful consideration, especially in the area of cost and expenses.

Traditional college and university systems charge a set tuition based on the number of course credits a student completes per semester. Usually there are fees associated with the cost of tuition, including building use fees, recreation costs, housing, and meal plans, just to mention a few. The assumption is made that a student who attends face-to-face classes walks on the grounds, lives in a dorm, and becomes part of the campus culture.

Because of the day-to-day activities and operations on a campus, institutions incur electrical costs, facilities repairs, transportation expenses, and general maintenance charges (Paul, 2013). Other financial sources, excluding funding associated with tuition and assessed fees, are derived from grants, donations, and of course, state and federal agencies. Facing these costs and more, the days of a student walking on a campus are numbered. Online learning may well be the most efficient way for a student to obtain a college degree.

Online programs from accredited colleges and universities are often reasonably priced, alleviate travel costs, provide outreach to remote locations, and allow working professionals some flexibility and convenience when completing their courses of study (Farmer & Weber, 2009, p. 2). Financial considerations and the effective use of time may have more of an impact on school choice than traditions or family lineage.

Take for instance the University of Phoenix. This university is accredited and serves approximately 400,000 students at any given time (Paul, 2013). The university maintains no centralized or permanent brick-and-mortar location and rents most of the spaces actually used by the school (Paul, 2013). There is no comparison between the daily costs of operating a rented facility and those of running an on-the-ground campus. Students could very well see this type of savings reflected in tuition costs or associated fees.

To stay alive in the competitive market of higher education, traditional institutions must face and embrace the online movement before they become extinct. Many low-enrollment colleges and universities have already succumbed to this "steamroller" impact of online learning and found they were unable to move forward. Paul (2013) points out that larger institutions such as Harvard, MIT, Berkeley, Georgetown, Wellesley, and the University of Texas have incorporated online components in several of their program offerings (p. 108). He also insists that if these prestigious colleges and universities have accepted this paradigm shift and are responding to it, online education is most definitely becoming a valid means to achieve a college degree.

Even with the onset and growing readiness to offer degree programs online, Carey (2015) contends that traditional colleges and universities are still experiencing a constant enrollment. However, Carey (2015) also draws attention to the fact that tuition costs and student loans are higher than in the past. With these facts in place, two important questions rise to the surface for an on-the-ground education system:

1. What will brick-and-mortar schools have to do to remain financially solvent?
2. How will brick-and-mortar schools shift financial expenditures in such a way as to continue providing a quality education for their students?

To stay financially solvent, colleges and universities rely on many outside sources for their funding means, and many times these monies are dedicated to specific spending areas such as faculty and staff salaries. A budget process is in place that allows departments and programs a certain number of "lines." These lines usually refer to the faculty members that are allowed, through the budget process, in their departments. With online education, the number of actual full-time faculty members may be affected.

The cost of employing a full-time faculty member includes not only salary but also insurance, benefits, federal tax expenditures, and facilities use. If online education is becoming the norm in lieu of on-the-ground education, adjunct faculty may be a consideration for some institutions as they seek ways to be more cost-efficient in their spending. Full-time faculty may find themselves adjusting to more than changes in delivery methods.

Another consideration for colleges and universities is the fact that an online education actually would reduce the use of buildings, maintenance of the grounds, and number of student-related events that take place at any given time on a campus. All of this would help defer certain costs at the college level.

Having an online presence does not mean that traditional colleges and universities add money to their coffers. Expenditures on providing a quality education are still part of the college system; however, with an online education, differing costs emerge.

Downes (2004) mentions that the costs of an online degree program include (1) constant technological support through personnel and provider systems, (2) employment of product developers, (3) continual upgrades to hardware mechanisms, and (4) a sophisticated management system (pp. 22–23).

Another consideration is how the use of the Internet places current and reliable information into the hands of any learner anywhere. Most of these sources are free of charge, and this quite possibly could mean savings for a college or university when examining the ways the library system is being used on a campus (Wilen-Daugenti, 2009). E-books would replace hardbound books and reduce the space needed in a library. Libraries would no longer order magazine and journal subscriptions because those sources could be found online at a reduced cost.

Providing a college degree online is not the wave of the future. It is the reality of the present. Those seeking a college degree to improve their personal and professional lives have a variety of institutions from which to choose. Financial considerations are imperative for institutions of higher learning as they strive to stay current as well as keep their doors open with the online phenomenon taking place.

COST TO THE STUDENTS

There is no discounting the fact that an online education from an accredited institution, in many cases, is less expensive than the traditional method of earning a college degree. Students seeking a college degree save money on travel and fees associated with campus life and housing, all the while staying employed at their jobs. Affordability and accessibility are offered to those who seek a college degree but do not have the means to achieve that goal. An online program provides them with that vehicle.

Institutions that maintain a quality online program utilize technological resources that place experts in a field of study into living rooms instead of lecture halls, provide formidable lectures through various streaming methods, initiate conversations from around the world, and are attentive to "hands-on learning no matter where [a student] is located" (Wilen-Daugenti, 2009, p. 3).

While the online delivery method may not be the perfect fit for all, this format does allow those students with other educational concerns, such as those with few financial or human resources, dropouts or homebound students, and those who live in desolate or rural communities (Henig & Hess, 2010, p. 60), to extend their collegiate possibilities.

However, future college-bound students and their families must not be swayed by all the promises made by online college or university programs. There are some hidden costs to students that are not always revealed in advertisements or glossy flyers. Questions should be asked about the "real" price of textbooks, outside fees for additional links to run certain programs, and what certifications will be earned from the program.

Online educational programs offer a wide assortment of degrees; however, many do not offer the certification that is required for a degree. For instance, several online universities offer master's degrees in the field of educational leadership for those students seeking a principalship. A graduate will complete all the courses necessary to meet the requirements of that degree. Because online programs cannot provide state-specific certifications, the principal candidate must now seek an accredited college, university, or state entity to complete the state requirements for licensure. This means that to become state certified a student will incur additional costs to meet his or her desired professional goal.

Not all costs to students are monetary. There is also an emotional price to pay when taking online courses, as students could experience the loss of a personal connection to their college or university. Traditions associated with college life are experienced at the campus, not through computers or accessing the Internet. The freshman year of college for on-the-ground students helps them develop lasting friendships that might be lost while meeting in a "chat room."

Relationships that grow between a professor and a student over a four-year period at traditional institutions become less important. Networking skills and the possibility of a professional recommendation are only two of the losses students may experience in choosing an online education instead of a face-to-face learning method.

Price (2008) warns that online education, while cost-efficient in some cases, also equates to a "loss of a human face in learning" (para. 8). He also comments on how this kind of disconnected learning through a computer prevents certain forms of needed communication. Those students who choose a profession such as teaching, which definitely requires effective communication skills, may experience feelings of isolation through the online delivery method (Price, 2008). A degree will be earned but at what emotional price to the student?

Wilen-Daugenti (2009) believes that while student engagement is certainly experienced differently by an online learner, purposeful communications and intentional conversations such as those experienced by on-the-ground learners are now slowly ebbing as technology overcomes the need to be a part of a traditional college institution. Cost, time, and flexibility outweigh the need to watch a basketball game, join a sorority, or even meet at the library for a study group.

CONCLUSION

Technological advancements have streamlined and improved day-to-day life and on-the-job responsibilities for many professions. Some new gadget or apparatus is outdated even before the long line of people waiting to purchase one gets to the front door of Best Buy. Telecommunication sources have surpassed a simple phone line and moved to watches that speak and read emails. These are only two examples of how technology has improved lives and made things a little easier for some. However, with these advancements and more, a question arises as to what the real cost is, especially in higher education.

Earning a four-year degree from an accredited college or university still opens doors to a professional world. The completion of a degree means that a candidate has met certain standards and expectations of a prescribed program of study. Whether online or face-to-face, the education and learning acquired by students meet certain accreditation standards that deem them employable. To ensure these remain a part of the higher education system, policies and practices must be in place.

Online programs present various challenges where policies are concerned. Henig and Hess (2010) hold that with online courses, policies are required to ensure that educational and accreditation standards are upheld, promises of a quality education are maintained, and local control of the educational process is intact.

Policies that govern academic honesty, attendance and participation, and students needing modification must be defined in accordance with the use of technology. Henig and Hess (2010) remind colleges and universities that while technology certainly changes the pace of the educational system, these technologies also "require new political arrangements, government transparency, and . . . policies if they are to deliver on their promises" (p. 60).

A professor who used to explain his or her class syllabus during a face-to-face meeting now uploads said syllabus as part of the online content and hopes students read the vital information, hence creating the possibility of miscommunicating required information about existing policies found in a syllabus.

With the current economic conditions and the continued realization that to be successful in a chosen profession, a college degree is still the path most taken, online learning may be the only viable solution for some because of time-related constraints, the ability to move at one's own speed through the content, and the promise of a college education at a fraction of the cost to attend a traditional institution.

Many colleges and universities will have to rethink not only the way their education is delivered but the way monies are spent. Technology presents a very different means of attaining a college degree that will only continue to grow and expand within an educational system. Perna et al. (2014) make the point that institutions of higher learning will incur the cost of "expand[ing] access and opportunities for all students to participate in and benefit from higher education [while reducing the cost to the students]" (p. 421).

KEY POINTS

- Policies aid and guide colleges and universities in focusing on the implementation and assessment of quality online programs.
- Institutions of higher education must remain constantly aware of state and federal guidelines regarding their financial status. Where online or on-the-ground programs are concerned, awareness of initial, maintenance, and hidden costs is essential.
- Online education offered by colleges and universities must stay up-to-date on any new and evolving technologies to remain competitive in a highly competitive arena.

REFERENCES

Bidwell, A. (2014, October 30). Education department's gainful employment rules rebuffed. *U.S. News and World Report*. Retrieved from https://www.usnews.com/news/articles/2014/10/30/obama-administration-gainful-employment-rules-upset-student-groups-for-profits.

Burnsed, B. (2011, April 20). Online education may transform higher education. *U.S. News & World Report*. Retrieved from https://www.usnews.com/education/online-education-may-transform-higher-ed.

Carey, K. (2015, March 8). Here's what will truly change higher education: Online degrees that are seen as official. *New York Times*. Retrieved from https://www.nytimes.com/2015/03/08/upshot/true-reform-in-higher-education-when-online-degrees-are-seen-as-official:html?_r=08.

Cook, V., & Kubatzke, K. (2007, June). Teaching and learning in an online degree program: A review of one program. *International Journal of Educational Leadership Preparation, 2*(1). Retrieved from http://www.ncpeapublications.org/index.php/volume-2-number-1-january-june-2007/297-teaching-and-learning-in-an-online-degree-program-a-review-of-one-program-.

Downes, S. (2004). Learning objectives: Resources for learning worldwide. In R. McGreal (ed.), *Online education using learning objectives* (pp. 21–31). New York, NY: Routledge Falmer.

Farmer, T. A., & Weber, M. J. (2009). *Evolution or extinction: Online leadership preparation programs*. Paper presented at the annual meeting of the National Council of Professors of Educational Leadership, San Antonio, TX.

Fowler, F. C. (2004). *Policy studies for educational leaders: An introduction*. 2nd ed. Upper Saddle River, NJ: Pearson.

Henig, J. R., & Hess, F. M. (2010, November). The declining significance of space and geography. *Kappan 92*(3), 57–61.

Paul, R. (2013). *The school revolution: A new answer for our broken education system*. New York, NY: Grand Central.

Perna, L. W., Ruby, A., Boruch, R. F., Wang, N., Scull, J., Ahmad, S., & Evans, C. (2014, December). Moving through MOOCs: Understanding the progression of users in massive open online courses. *Educational Researcher 43*(9), 421–432.

Price, W. J. (2008, June 11). The impending death of face-to-face instruction: Notes from a Neo-Luddite. *Education Week*. Retrieved from http://www.edweek.org/ew/articles/2008/06/11/41price_ep.h27.html?tkn=ULRF5KjFDbpqlvv8NgxoHI.

Romano, L. (2006, May 15). Online degree programs take off. *Washington Post*. Retrieved from http://www.washingtonpost.com/wp-dyn/content/articles/2006/05/15/AR2006051501496_pf.html.

Tareilo, J. (2009). *Readying instructors for classrooms without walls: The impact of online learning for professors and their programs*. Paper presented at the annual meeting of the National Council of Professors of Educational Administration, San Antonio, TX.

Texas Higher Education Coordinating Board. (n.d.). *Distance education policies, procedures, and forms*. Retrieved from http://www.thecb.state.tx.us/index.cfm?objectid=A5A15ZAC-D290-334F-87262E9E77B3B37.

Watson, J. (2008, Fall). *Online learning: The national landscape*. Retrieved from www.ciconline.org/threshold.

Wilen-Daugenti, T. (2009). *.edu: Technology and learning environments in higher education*. New York, NY: Peter Lang.

11

WHAT TO LOOK FOR WHEN HIRING A CANDIDATE TRAINED ONLINE

Stacy Hendricks

As searches begin for teaching and administrative positions, it is important that the individuals with hiring authority understand that candidates who have received online certification may be just as qualified, or even more qualified, than those with face-to-face training. In most instances, all candidates have participated in a variety of education preparation programs.

The delivery method among the programs may have been face-to-face, blended/hybrid, or completely online. However, hiring decisions regarding campus teachers and district leaders should not be based on the program delivery method; instead, decisions should be based on the leadership qualities, or skill set, the candidate possesses.

Many individuals hiring candidates trained online continue to be skeptical of the online programs; however, when examining job descriptions for teaching and administrative positions, most online candidates are adequately qualified for the posted positions. Obviously, no matter what type of program the candidate completes, whether it is face-to-face or online, he or she must complete the necessary steps to obtain the state certification for the particular position, be it teaching or administrative.

For administrators, this will most likely be a master's degree that includes coursework and practicum hours, and, finally, the candidate must pass the state testing requirements. For teachers, in addition to the coursework, practicum hours, and certification exams, one would conclude coursework by student teaching and then he or she would obtain a bachelor's degree.

Beyond the required state certification, job descriptions consistently sought other assets such as strong communication, public relations, interpersonal skills, collaboration, and problem-solving skills. Of course, the administrative job descriptions went into further detail explaining specific responsibilities under each area.

Regardless of the delivery method or program, it is important that professors remain aware of the needs of those hiring the students. The teaching or educational leadership program is only as good as the students that are getting hired for the teaching or administrative positions. Therefore, it behooves the professors in these programs to determine what is needed for a candidate searching for the teaching or administrative position.

Then, the professors can align those needs with the state standards of the educational program as well as district needs. Intertwining the two, candidates are prepared for both the state certification and the "real" world. If the courses in the program are designed effectively, the delivery method should not matter.

Online students, whether in the teacher education program or the educational leadership program, improve in many areas, which may include but are not limited to (1) communication skills, both oral and written; (2) technological skills; (3) ability to handle constructive criticism; (4) collaboration; (5) self-discipline and self-motivation; (6) self-starter and deadline oriented; and (7) problem-solving skills.

Although this is a great list of qualities, it is not all-encompassing. Though there are many other qualities that candidates from online programs possess, these seven qualities will be discussed in this chapter.

COMMUNICATION SKILLS

First, an effective teacher or leader must possess strong communication skills. After all, in order to teach or lead a campus, the individual must be able to communicate with a variety of people or groups of people such as the students, faculty, parents, superintendent, school board, and community organizations.

For example, at any given time, the principal may need to communicate with the stakeholders by writing letters, memos, or emails; thus, effective written communication is certainly needed. Also, a teacher is continuously writing emails and letters to parents, as well as producing work for students, which must model proper language usage.

However, the teacher or principal frequently must speak to different groups of individuals, so it is equally important that he sharpen his oral communication skills. Faculty meetings, parent-teacher conferences, school board meetings, parent-teacher organizations, student assemblies, and community events are just a few opportunities in which strong oral communication skills are needed. Therefore, it is without argument that an effective teacher or principal must possess strong communication skills.

As graduates of an online program, administrative candidates have had ample opportunity to enhance their communication skills. In online courses, most of the communication between the students and the professor as well as among students is written. As stated by Thiede (2012), "Online courses can offer a much greater opportunity than face-to-face classes for students to write in a reflective manner, analyze information and materials and conduct research" (p. 140).

The most common way to communicate in an online class is through email. Many issues arise from written communication in emails. People tend to infer more from an email than is meant by the author, or a "certain" tone is inferred from the email that was not necessarily intended. This is also true with chats or online discussions. Therefore, the students must learn to construct the wording of emails very carefully in order to prevent potential problems with the professor as well as other students.

Additionally, many assignments given in online courses may ask students to reflect on personal experiences, summarize articles, respond to teaching or leadership scenarios, and/or complete a research project. The students must hone their written communication skills in order to complete these assignments and communicate effectively.

The professor will provide constructive feedback regarding content as well as grammatical issues on these written assignments. Then, the student will be given the opportunity to correct the deficiencies. Given the feedback and the second opportunity, students will learn from their mistakes and become better at written communication through online programs.

Students not only communicate by writing to the professors but may also communicate orally. A professor has designated office hours for the purpose of helping students. Therefore, a student has the capability to contact the professor by phone during those hours. When contacting a professor, it is important that the student give a good impression.

Thus, the student must use correct grammar. He must have done his "homework" before he calls the professor. In other words, the phone call must have a purpose, and the student is responsible for being knowledgeable about and articulating understanding of the topic that the phone call is regarding. Being prepared to speak on a topic is one characteristic that is needed in a leader. While speaking, articulating the topic well and using correct grammar is a must.

Some students may not need to directly contact the professor. However, online classes provide additional ways to develop oral communication skills in students. In some online courses, assignments are completed using audio. For example, the student will be asked to answer a scenario by using the audio capability in the online program framework. Additionally, another assignment may ask a student to complete a video presentation.

For instance, the student may be asked to make a professional development presentation for the first day of school. The professor would give the guidelines to include a visual presentation as well as a video of the student conducting the professional development. This assignment actually incorporates both the oral and written communication.

With such assignments, online students continue to hone their oral and written communication skills. In sum, "online courses promote the constructivist model of education and encourage more individualized student communication which is advantageous in the learning process" (Schell & Janicki, 2013, p. 34).

TECHNOLOGICAL SKILLS

Second, an online student will possess technological proficiency. The online student will be given multiple opportunities to advance his or her technology skills. In fact, just completing an online course increases one's technology knowledge. However, in the online courses, students are faced with other advanced technology that they may or may not be familiar with. Students must first familiarize themselves with the online course framework such as Blackboard or Desire2Learn. Once in the course, the student must become knowledgeable of the course components.

Email, chat, discussion boards, viewing content and grades, taking quizzes, and uploading assignments are just a few of the basic components that the online student must master during the online course. Then, there are other technology skills that specific assignments require.

For example, students must be able to use Word, PowerPoint, and Excel. Other assignments include more advanced technology such as audio and video production. Particular assignments such as this may require the student to use a webcam, a microphone, and an online recording program such as Screencast-O-Matic.

When surveyed, a student was asked how his technological proficiency had improved over the semester of the online class. He stated, "Tenfold—I've become proficient with many programs, learned to do stuff like screencasts, and have even begun leading my students in class in blogging and using Twitter."

If a student learns something new in an online class and transfers the "new" learning to his own classroom, there is no doubt that particular candidate will use the technology to lead the school and, equally important, teach others in the school how to use the technology to improve student learning.

CONSTRUCTIVE CRITICISM

Third, constructive criticism is something that one continues to receive throughout life. There is always someone that can and will provide you with constructive criticism. If handled correctly, the feedback can make the skill set of an individual that much better. However, if the individual does nothing with the feedback, then nothing will be gained. Lessons can always be learned from mistakes.

Thus, in an online learning environment, professors provide students with constructive feedback in order to improve their teaching or leadership skill set. Koohang, Smith, Yerby, and Floyd (2012) agreed, noting that assignments and activities should be followed up with assessments and feedback in order to determine whether learning has occurred and to what extent. The program goes beyond the actual grade; instead, the online learning environment provides the opportunity for professors to critique each student's work. Then, individually, the student will be given feedback.

In some instances, the student may be allowed to resubmit the assignment, thus providing another learning opportunity for the student. Either way, the student receives individual feedback on assignments that allows for reflection and improvement in leadership areas such as problem solving and written communication.

Therefore, when online administrative candidates begin their first principal position, not only can they apply the feedback that they have already been given by the professor, but they will also know how to use future constructive criticism to improve in their principal position. Likewise, from the constructive criticism of the professor, the teacher candidate can reflect on the lessons learned and apply the new techniques and knowledge to his or her classroom.

COLLABORATION

Fourth, the ability to collaborate with others is another quality that an online candidate will possess. While face-to-face courses incorporate collaboration, it is much more important in an online course. Otherwise, the online course turns into nothing more than a correspondence course. While discussion boards are important, it is even more important for students to work together. This can be very difficult for an online course. However, it certainly can be done.

Within the course, assignments are often given as group assignments where students gather in pairs or groups and begin collaborating on certain research topics or educational issues. The students are left to decide how and when they will collaborate. They can use the chat capability, discussion board, or email, or they may decide to use other technology such as FaceTime or Skype.

In most cases, the logistics of how and when do not really matter; instead, the focus should be on the time working together and the end product that is achieved through a collaborative approach. Richardson and Swan (2003) stated, "Some theorists characterize learning as an interactive group process in which the learners actively construct knowledge and then build upon that knowledge through the exchange of ideas with others and the responses/feedback of others" (p. 80).

Collaborating on assignments allows the students to gain other perspectives (i.e., secondary vs. elementary, small district vs. large district, etc.). Then, whenever they get a job in unfamiliar territory, they will have past experiences from their collaboration with their colleagues.

Equally important, the students will have made contacts with other individuals in the profession. The collaboration "buddies" will be able to provide support and resources for each other. Lastly, collaboration creates the opportunity for individuals to work with various personalities, learning styles, and ability levels.

More than likely, in an online course, collaboration takes place among students who do not know each other. In face-to-face courses, it is likely that through the sequence of courses, students begin to get familiar with each other. However, in an online course, the likelihood of students working with someone they know is low.

Thus, the online course adds another level to the collaboration among students. Realistically, when a teacher or principal takes a position at a new school, he must begin collaborating with those on his campus. In most instances, he will not know the individuals; accordingly, this is another example of how the online candidate will be prepared by experiences, activities, and assignments in an online class.

SELF-DISCIPLINE AND SELF-MOTIVATION

Fifth, a student in an online class must be self-disciplined and self-motivated. These qualities must be student driven. In most online courses, professors have planned the course in advance. Consequently, the students can usually view the material for the entire semester. The assignments are visible as well as the due dates. It is up to the online student to be disciplined enough to begin the work well in advance of the due date to complete all of the necessary assignments.

Since there is not a set class time, this is difficult for some students. For reasons such as family commitments, work, and personal life, some online students do not complete their course or program. In other words, the online student must be self-disciplined and self-motivated to get the assignments completed on time.

This does not mean that the student must forget about his family, work, and personal life. Instead, it means that he must organize and compartmentalize his time, be disciplined about getting the work done in all areas, and anticipate and have contingencies for unexpected delays.

Not only should the student be self-disciplined with time, but he should also be self-motivated. The online professor will not be the motivating factor in the class. That is left up to the online student. In face-to-face courses, oftentimes, the professors are attempting to motivate through lectures or through face-to-face activities.

However, in an online course, the student must have the internal motivation to want to learn. The material is presented in various ways; however, the online students must be self-motivated to learn the material.

The old adage "You will get out what you put in" comes to mind with online courses. The more disciplined and motivated you are to learn, the more you will learn. When taking a new position in a school district, educators are asked to do many things, such as improve test scores, improve retention rates, improve the gifted and talented program, etc. In order to make improvements on a campus, the educator must be motivated to do so.

However, motivation cannot be the only factor; one must be self-disciplined. To expect others to be motivated and disciplined within their work, one must lead by example. Online courses require students to be self-disciplined and self-motivated in order to survive the course. Thus, when online students actually become teachers and principals they can lead by example because of what they have learned and experienced in their online courses.

SELF-STARTER AND DEADLINE ORIENTED

Sixth, a student in an online course must be a self-starter and deadline oriented. These two characteristics go hand in hand with self-discipline and self-motivation. After all, one must be motivated to get started! In an online course, there is not a professor to remind you to get started on the assignment that is due next week. Instead, the due dates are listed and the expectation is that you will get started in plenty of time to complete a quality assignment and get it submitted by the due date.

The advantage of an online class is flexibility. You can work on assignments when you want. One student may start several days or weeks ahead of another student in the same class. Therefore, it is not realistic for the professor to tell students when to get started on assignments. Instead, the due date is listed and it is up to the student to get started in time to complete the assignment. For that reason, the online student must be a self-starter.

Along the same lines, the online student knows the due dates for each of the assignments. The student must determine how and when he will get all of the assignments and quizzes completed. The bottom line is the deadline. The other logistics are left up to the student. Hence, it is important that the online student be a self-starter and deadline oriented. Otherwise, deadlines will be missed and grades will be penalized.

For an online professor, the expectation is that students will take the initiative to begin the assignments and follow deadlines in order to turn in quality work on time. For an educator in K–12, the expectations are the same for the elementary and secondary students. The difference is the classroom environment and the pedagogical approach.

In the K–12 environment or a face-to-face university setting, the teacher or professor is there to prompt and guide the student from the starting phase through to the final product. In an online course, the professor is more like a facilitator. He may send reminders through emails, chats, and discussions; however, the student is in a completely different location and it is up to the student to get started and meet the deadline.

In the real world, there is no one there to guide you along the way. You are given a deadline to make something happen and you need to get started well in advance to make it happen by that date. The same is true with a teacher or principal at a school.

The state testing deadline is not fluid. Therefore, you cannot wait until a week before the state tests and decide to develop a plan for academic improvement. This simply will not work. Online courses offer students opportunities to initiate projects and meet specific deadlines.

Being a self-starter and deadline oriented will be beneficial in everyday life, and especially for a campus teacher or district leader.

PROBLEM SOLVING

Finally, problem solving is another quality needed in a teacher or leader. As one enters the field of education, it is imperative that he be able to solve problems. Throughout online classes, students are given scenarios that provide them with the opportunity to solve a situational problem as if they were in the "real" world.

In some instances, the way one student answers the question may be different than another student. Then, a class discussion occurs regarding the varying ideas. This tends to stretch the students' thinking.

It is imperative that students begin solving problems early in the online program. In addition to scenarios and other class assignments, online students have other opportunities to improve on their problem-solving skills. In fact, the entire program tests these skills.

For example, when a student begins the online program, they may not have taken any previous online courses. Therefore, entering into the course and maneuvering through the discussion posts, chats, emails, Dropbox, etc., can cause immediate problems. However, it is up to the student to figure out how to operate the functions of the class.

Then, as assignments are given, more technology is added and again, it is up to the student to determine how to complete the assignment using the specific technology requested. For example, in a couple of the author's classes, the students must use the audio capability to complete their assignment.

In another class, the students must create a visual presentation and capture themselves on video completing a presentation to a campus. Most of the students have not used this type of technology. Therefore, they must use their "problem-solving" skills to complete the assignment successfully.

An online program instills problem-solving skills in principal preparation students through assignments and scenarios as well as through the technology and individualized online classroom setting. While the qualities mentioned above may also be found in a student that has completed face-to-face courses, online courses have been developed in such a way that online students have experienced activities and assignments that enhance these qualities within each individual student.

Strong communication skills, technological skills, constructive criticism, collaboration, self-discipline, self-motivation, the ability to be a self-starter and deadline oriented, and problem solving are all important lifelong skills needed for all individuals, and beginning a career with these qualities will certainly provide a principal or teacher candidate with the necessary skills and credentials to effectively lead a campus.

Through assignments, chats, discussion boards, and quizzes, online courses provide students with opportunities to develop and hone certain skills or qualities that will be beneficial not only to the administrative and teaching candidates looking for a position but also to the employer who hires them.

HIRING THE "RIGHT" PERSON

Hiring the "right" person for the position is a crucial task. It is important that the individual or committee responsible for hiring make certain that the individual hired is the "right" individual for the job! It is also necessary to ensure that the candidate has the skill set to successfully complete the job. It is important that those hiring look for specific qualifications in candidates.

While online candidates have had many opportunities to develop a variety of skills while in the online program, it is left up to those hiring to determine the level of each skill within the individual candidates. In order to do this, those with hiring authority might want to determine whether online candidates are equally qualified as traditional candidates.

With online candidates, it is important to ask direct questions to determine whether they are qualified for the available teaching or administrative position. Those with hiring authority may ask the candidates to discuss such areas as their teaching and practicum experiences, professional growth activities, community involvement activities, and any additional artifacts. Each online student should have worked with a mentor and completed many valuable practicum activities in a variety of areas that align with state and national standards.

The student should be able to articulate specific activities that he participated in during the educator preparation program. Additionally, an online candidate should be able to discuss professional growth activities. This should include professional development activities related to the principal as well as in the classroom. Another component required in the graduate online program is participation in community activities. Through practicum activities and assignments, online students are required to have interaction with community stakeholders.

During the interview process, the online administrative candidate should be able to speak about the involvement of community stakeholders from personal experience. For example, the candidate may be able to discuss a communication plan that he has written. He may be able to discuss PTO meetings, board meetings, or involvement with other organizations such as the Lions Club or Rotary.

Lastly, an online candidate should be able to produce artifacts of a variety of activities. This portfolio may include examples of the specific qualities that he possesses that would make him a "fit" for the available position. Through the artifacts, those with the hiring authority will be able to glean valuable information to determine whether the online candidate is the "right" person for the job.

The portfolio should be a well-rounded document that provides the hiring committee with an opportunity to see the knowledge and skills the candidate possesses. Also, this document will demonstrate a lot about the individual. After looking through artifacts or a portfolio, those hiring might want to ponder the following questions when interviewing a candidate:

- How has the candidate communicated effectively?
- What technological skills does the candidate possess?
- How does he or she demonstrate the ability to handle constructive criticism?
- Using specific examples, describe collaboration.
- How has your online program prepared you to be self-disciplined or self-motivated? How is it applicable to the role of the teacher or principal?
- How has your online program prepared you to be a self-starter and deadline oriented? How is it applicable to the role of the teacher or principal?

- Describe two examples from your online practicum that required you to use your problem-solving skills.

After visiting with the online candidate and looking through the portfolio, those with the hiring authority should be able to determine whether that candidate possesses the necessary experiences and skills to move their campus to the next level.

CONCLUSION

While hiring is a tough job, it has been made more difficult over the past decade due to the vast number of students completing their education preparation program online. As noted in chapters 4 and 9, many individuals with hiring authority have been skeptical of online programs.

However, the online program should not be the cause of the skepticism; instead, the skeptics should be concerned with placing the "right" person in the "right" position. In order to determine the placement, one must look past whether the program was face-to-face or online. Instead, hiring administrators need to look at the qualities and skill set that each individual brings to the position.

For the aforementioned reasons, online candidates are just as prepared through experiences such as assignments, field experiences, discussions, chats, collaborative activities, and scenarios as any face-to-face candidate. In fact, one might argue that online candidates might be more prepared in certain areas than candidates who received their certification via traditional methods of delivery. In sum, it is up to hiring administrators to look past the delivery method of the program and focus on the individual qualities of each candidate. As Baghdadi (2011) stated, "what matters is the high quality of learning, whether that learning is offered on campus or via the Internet" (p. 115).

KEY POINTS

- Regardless of the delivery method, the quality of learning is of utmost importance.

- When hiring, focus on the quality of the individual rather than the delivery method of the educator preparation program.
- When interviewing, questions must be developed to delve into the quality of the educational preparation program.
- There must be a mind shift in those hiring, to understand that online programs and courses can offer as many great educational experiences as face-to-face courses.

REFERENCES

Baghdadi, Z. D. (2011, July). Best practices in online education: Online instructors, courses, and administrators. *Turkish Online Journal of Distance Education 12*(3), 109–117.

Koohang, A., Smith, T., Yerby, J., & Floyd, K. (2012). Active learning in online courses: An examination of students' learning experience. *International Journal of Management, Knowledge and Learning 1*(2), 205–216.

Richardson, J. C., & Swan, K. (2003, February). Examining social presence in online courses in relation to students' perceived learning and satisfaction. *Journal of Asynchronous Learning Networks 7*(1), 68–88.

Schell, G. P., & Janicki, T. J. (2013, Winter). Online course pedagogy and the constructivist learning model. *Journal of the Southern Association for Information Systems 1*(1). doi:http://dx.doi.org/10.3998/jsais.11880084.0001.104.

Thiede, R. (2012). Best practices with online courses. *US-China Education Review, A2*, 135–141.

12

THE SIGNIFICANCE OF ONLINE LEARNING TO K–12 SETTINGS

Tracey Covington Hasbun

Online learning is a rapidly expanding approach in American educational settings. The U.S. Department of Education (USDE) states: "Online learning, for students and for teachers, is one of the fastest growing trends in educational uses of technology" (2010, p. xi). Also, according to an article in *U.S. News and World Report*, more online courses and programs are being offered in higher education in order to meet the needs of students with work and/or family commitments (Golod, 2014). Much like in higher education, there has also been increased enrollment in fully online public schools and in online learning in kindergarten through 12th grade (K–12).

According to the International Association for K–12 Online Learning (iNACOL) (2013a), approximately 200,000 students were enrolled in fully online schools, in kindergarten through 12th grade, during the 2009–2010 academic year. By 2011, that number increased to 275,000 students (iNACOL, 2013a). Only one year later, during the 2012–2013 school year, the number had risen to 310,000 students (iNACOL, 2013b).

In addition to students participating in fully online schools, over 1 million students in grades K–12 took some type of online course during the 2007–2008 school year (Picciano & Seaman, 2007). In a blog published by the Clayton Christensen Institute, it was also noted that more than 4 million K–12 students took a minimum of one online course (Horn, 2011). With such an increase in the number of fully online schools and with the large number of students taking at least one online course in some form, it is necessary to investigate the online phenomena in K–12.

What is involved in online learning? Is it good for our students in grades K–12? While some point to the flexibility of online learning and the benefits it provides to performers, athletes, military families, struggling students, and advanced learners, to name a few, others argue that there is no data to support online learning and that it is not accessible to all students (Gabriel, 2011; K12 Inc., 2014e). As education changes to meet the needs of students and as it prepares citizens for the future, having knowledge of the K–12 online trend is essential.

To begin with, it is important to understand the terms involved with K–12 online learning before "wading" into the world of online education. One reason is that some terms may sound very similar but may have very different meanings.

Additionally, it is important to understand the elements that comprise the K–12 online framework and to understand what is currently taking place in K–12 online learning. Finally, the benefits and concerns associated with learning in a K–12 online environment should be examined.

OVERVIEW OF TERMS

To date, there are various types of online learning offered in the K–12 setting. These diverse formats are also supported or administered by diverse entities. One might read about full-time online or virtual schools or might hear about blended learning.

Distance education might be a topic of discussion, along with concepts like multi-district fully online schools, state online schools, and synchronous or asynchronous learning. All of these different terms can be very confusing and can leave a person with more questions than answers regarding online learning in K–12.

Before an educator, parent or caregiver, administrator, or policy maker can have a clear sense of what is taking place in K–12 online learning, one must have a general understanding of some of the key terms involved. This is important as some terms may seem similar but can have very different meanings. Additionally, due to how quickly technology changes, new terms often arise. While the following list is not inclusive, it should provide a basis for what is discussed in this chapter.

Definition of Terms

- Asynchronous learning: "Communication exchanges which occur in elapsed time between two or more people. Examples are email, on-line discussion forums, message boards, blogs, podcasts, etc." (iNAC-OL, 2011, p. 3).
- Blended learning: A format in which students learn at least part of their content and instruction online, "with some element of student control over time, place, path, and/or pace." Blended learning "must be supervised and take place away from home" (Staker & Horn, 2012, p. 3). An example of blended online learning can be seen in the Milpitas Unified School District in California (Milpitas Unified School District, 2015).
- Blended schools: "Stand-alone schools with a school code (as opposed to programs within a school) that deliver much of their curriculum in a blended format and students are required to show up at a physical site for more than just state assessments" (Watson et al., 2013, p. 9).
- Distance education: "General term for any type of educational activity in which the participants are at a distance from each other—in other words, are separated in space. They may or may not be separated in time (asynchronous vs. synchronous)" (iNACOL, 2011, p. 5). Distance education or distance learning may encompass online learning or "earlier technologies such as correspondence courses, educational television and videoconferencing" (USDE, 2010, p. xi).
- Fully online schools: "These schools are often referred to as cyberschools and work with students who are enrolled primarily (often only) in the online school. Cyberschools typically are responsible for ensuring their students take state assessments, and are responsible for their students' scores on those assessments. Many fully online schools are charter schools, although there are a growing number of fully online district schools" (Watson et al., 2013, p. 9). An example of a fully online or virtual school can be seen at K12 Inc. (K12 Inc., 2014a).

- Multi-district online program: "Program administered by multiple districts, often in a formal consortium. Not to be confused with a program that is administered by a single district even though it accepts students from multiple districts" (Watson & Kalmon, 2005, p. 127).
- Online learning: "Education in which instruction and content are delivered primarily over the Internet (Watson & Kalmon, 2005, p. 127). This term is often "used interchangeably with Virtual learning, Cyber learning, e-learning" (iNACOL, 2011, p. 7).
- Online school: "A formally constituted organization (public, private, state, charter, etc.) that offers full-time education delivered primarily over the Internet" (iNACOL, 2011, p. 7).
- Part-time online program: "An online program that allows students to take less than a full load of online courses, as defined by local or state legal entities" (iNACOL, 2011, p. 8).
- Single-district online program: "Program administered by a single district and provided to students within that district" (Watson & Kalmon, 2005, p. 121).
- State virtual school: "Created by legislation or by a state-level agency, and/or administered by a state education agency, and/or funded by a state appropriation or grant for the purpose of providing online learning opportunities across the state" (Watson et al., 2010, p. 14). State virtual schools may also receive funding from federal grants or private foundation grants and may charge course fees in order to cover costs (Watson et al., 2010). An example of a state virtual school is the Florida Virtual School (Florida Virtual School, 2014).
- Supplemental online learning: "Provide[s] a small number of courses to students who are enrolled in a school separate from the online program" (Watson et al., 2011, p. 11).
- Synchronous learning: "Online learning in which the participants interact at the same time and in the same space" (iNACOL, 2011, p. 9).
- Virtual school: See *Online school.*

K–12 ONLINE FRAMEWORK

Dimensions

Along with understanding terms involved with K–12 online learning, it is also important to have a basic understanding of the dimensions and categories that comprise the K–12 online framework. Before a parent or caregiver can make an educated decision as to which program is best for his or her child, he or she should know that there is diversity in the dimensions of those programs.

For example, there is diversity in the types of learning formats associated with online learning, there are a large range of providers associated with online learning, and programs can vary in their comprehensiveness (Watson et al., 2011).

K–12 online programs can also differ in the audience that they reach, in the type of institutions they serve, in the location where the learning takes place, and in delivery of instruction (Watson et al., 2011). Additionally, there can be various entities that have operational control of the learning, and the type of instruction can be different, as can the age of the students that are served (Watson et al., 2011).

For example, some programs are fully online while others offer individual courses that can be taken in order to supplement instruction, such as for course credit recovery or for courses that are not offered locally (Watson et al., 2011). Program reach can range from the district level to the international level and programs can be governed by authorities such as the local board, the state, or an independent vendor (Watson et al., 2011). In order to further clarify the various dimensions of online programs and to differentiate between their key elements, Figure 12.1 is provided (Watson et al., 2011).

Categories

Watson et al. (2011) note that online programs can have multiple attributes. They combined those attributes into five categories: single-district programs, multi-district full-time schools, consortium programs, state virtual schools, and programs that secondary institutions operate (Watson et al., 2011).

The Defining Dimensions of Online Programs

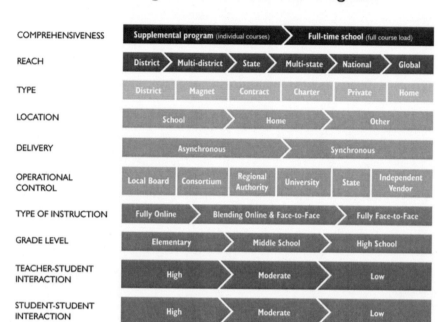

Figure adapted from Gregg Vanourek, A Primer on Virtual Charter Schools: Mapping the Electronic Frontier, Issue Brief for National Association of Charter School Authorizers, August 2006.

© Keeping Pace with K-12 Online Learning, 2011, kpk12.com

Figure 12.1.   The Defining Dimensions of Online Learning

They also organized categories of online programs into governance type, how the schools are funded, whether they are full-time or supplemental schools, and, again, the reach of the programs. Furthermore, they provided examples of actual schools from each category they created (Watson et al., 2011). Figure 12.2 provides a visual of the various categories.

CURRENT TRENDS AND PRACTICES

While terms can be helpful and having an understanding of the K–12 online framework is an important step in developing a basic under-

Categories of online programs					
Category	Organization type / governance	Full-time / supplemental	Funding source	Geographic reach	Examples
State virtual school	State education agency	Supplemental	State appropriation, course fees, funding formula	Statewide	Florida Virtual School, Michigan Virtual School, Idaho Digital Learning Academy
Multi-district	Charter or district-run	Full-time	Public education funding formula	Statewide	Oregon Connections Academy, Insight School of Washington, Georgia Virtual Academy, Minnesota Virtual High School
Single-district	District	Either or both	District funds	Single-district	Riverside (CA), Broward (FL), Plano (TX), Los Angeles, JeffCo (CO), WOLF (NV)
Consortium	Variable	Supplemental	Course fees, consortium member fees	Statewide, national, or global	Virtual High School Global Consortium, Wisconsin eSchool Network
Post-secondary	University or college	Either or both	Course fees	National	University of Nebraska Independent Study HS, Brigham Young University-Independent Study

© Keeping Pace with K-12 Online Learning, 2011, kpk12.com

Figure 12.2.   Categories of Online Learning

standing of the various types of learning offered online for K–12 students, it does not give a parent, caregiver, administrator, or teacher information regarding current trends and practices in K–12 online education. Current trends can provide stakeholders with information regarding options that are available.

In 2012, there were approximately 52 million public school students being educated in the United States (Center for Public Education, 2012). Of those 52 million students, it was indicated that only a small percentage were enrolled in online schools or in online classes (Center for Public Education, 2012). However, those numbers are increasing and "they are rapidly gaining ground" (Center for Public Education, 2012, p. 2).

Ambient Insight (2015) found that "while all domestic school systems are unique, the US stands out because it has the largest population of online PreK–12 students, so far. The large (and growing) number of children attending online primary and secondary schools fulltime in the US is a trend found nowhere else in the world" (p. 10). While Ambient Insight (2015) did not provide data on K–12, one could surmise that numbers could be relatively close to those found for PK–12.

Fully Online Schools

According to John Watson et al. (2014), there are 30 states in the U.S. that operate fully online schools in a K–12 setting. This allows students, in any portion of the state, to attend those online schools (Watson et al., 2014). They can be found in states such as Arizona, Colorado, Indiana, and Iowa (Watson et al., 2014). However, a full listing of available online learning options, by state, can be found in the Watson et al. (2014) annual report.

State Virtual Schools

There are also 26 states that have state virtual schools (Watson et al., 2014). These schools provide students across those states with the ability to take supplemental courses online (Watson et al., 2014). States such as Florida, Michigan, Idaho, and Georgia are noted for their state virtual schools (Watson et al., 2014). While fully online schools, also known as virtual schools, may sound very similar to state virtual schools, it is important to note the use of the term "state" in state virtual schools. A representative from iNACOL explained how these two terms vary:

> State virtual schools refer to schools that are governed by public entities like public school districts, independent and non-profit charter school boards, and state education agencies. The use of "state" in state virtual schools is an important distinction. . . . Otherwise, virtual schools and online schools can be used synonymously. Online schools can be non-profit and for profit, and more generally refer to online education providers—some are accredited, employ certified instructors, and some are neither. (M. Peterson, personal communication, January 15, 2015)

Course Choice Programs

Along with fully online and state virtual schools, there are also 11 states that provide course choice programs (Watson et al., 2014). These programs provide students with the option to choose online courses from several providers (Watson et al., 2014).

These programs can be found in states such as Florida, Utah, Louisiana, and Texas and "are particularly important, as they are the first significant effort to provide students the option to choose from multiple providers at the course level" (Watson et al., 2014, p. 5).

Distance Education Courses

Outside of fully online schools, state virtual schools, and course choice programs, there is also the availability of distance education courses for students in K–12. In 2009–2010, it was estimated that 1,816,400 enrollments were documented in distance education courses in school districts serving students in grades K–12 (iNACOL, 2013b).

Of those enrollments, approximately 74% were in high schools (iNACOL, 2013b). Online courses that experienced the greatest enrollment was due to students needing recovery of course credits, participating in dual enrollment, and taking advanced placement courses (iNACOL, 2013b).

Online Learning in Traditional Schools

Due to the inundation of technology in our society, even students in traditional brick-and-mortar schools are participating in some form of online learning. Students as young as five years old are engaging in online instruction through the use of literacy and math games within kindergarten classrooms. Elementary school students learn about computers and other uses of technology when they visit the school computer lab as part of their elective rotations.

Some high schools have mandated that online learning be a part of the curriculum. Several states, such as Michigan, Florida, Alabama, Virginia, and Arkansas, have decided that online learning should be one of the requirements for high school graduation (iNACOL, 2013b).

Clearly, online learning in grades K–12 in the United States is gaining ground. However, there is a debate as to whether or not this type of education is best for students and all educational stakeholders.

ARGUMENTS FOR AND AGAINST ONLINE LEARNING IN K–12

According to Gary Miron et al. (2013), in a brief for the National Education Policy Center, there are those that tout the benefits of K–12 online learning and those that are against this approach. Those in favor argue the quality of instruction can be improved while the cost of instruction can be decreased (Miron et al., 2013).

In contrast, there are those that contend a large portion of taxpayer money is directed to online learning and that there is not solid evidence to indicate the effectiveness of this approach (Miron et al., 2013). Arguments for and against online learning in K–12 deserve further examination.

Pros

Proponents of online education provide several reasons why they believe this instructional approach to be of value. Some point to the power of choice and the options that are available while others like the flexibility that online learning affords (Babson Survey Research Group, 2015; University of California Institute for Democracy, Education, and Access [UCLA IDEA], 2013). There are those who feel that online learning will provide children with access to highly qualified teachers and more one-on-one or individualized instruction (iNACOL, 2010; K12 Inc., 2014a).

Furthermore, some argue that, in light of finances and budget cuts, online classes are a way to reduce costs and still provide courses and credits that students need (UCLA IDEA, 2013). With many states and school districts being asked to do more with less, there are those that view online learning as more cost-effective, as opposed to traditional instruction that is provided in a brick-and-mortar institution.

Choice and Individualization

To begin with, many parents or caregivers feel that online learning can provide them with choices or options that may not be available in traditional K–12 schools. They can select a school, program, or instructional delivery format that best suits their child's needs and the unique needs of their family. These needs could be due to the learning style of the child, the acceleration of the child's learning, medical need, or other more personal preferences and/or issues.

First, students who have certain learning styles or who need individual pacing in their learning could benefit from an online K–12 setting. For example, a student who prefers learning in an environment with minimal distractions might find success with this type of learning format (K12 Inc., 2014d).

Additionally, students who require additional time to master a concept or students who are advanced, and might become bored with curriculum that is being provided in the traditional classroom, could find an online environment more conducive to their needs (K12 Inc., 2014c; 2014d).

Second, some feel that online learning allows schools to provide courses that might not otherwise be available (Huffington Post, 2011). If a student needs course credit recovery or wants to enroll in advanced placement courses or electives that are not offered at a local school, that is one benefit of online learning (Huffington Post, 2011). This is particularly important since an article in the *New York Times* indicated the fastest growth in online learning "has been in makeup courses for students who failed a regular class" (Gabriel, 2011, p. 2).

Third, online learning in grades K–12 could be a necessity for some students, due to medical need. The need could be a serious illness, a chronic illness, or an injury that prevents the student from attending a traditional school. Dealing with doctor's appointments and treatments could be challenging enough without the stress of trying to make up several weeks or months of missed academics (Pearson, 2015). By engaging in online learning, students with medical needs have an alternative to education that is only provided in a traditional brick-and-mortar institution.

Finally, there are parents and caregivers who find online learning in K–12 best for their child due to personal choices or personal issues that the family is facing. For example, if a parent or caregiver is concerned about gun violence, bullying, or overall safety in schools, he or she might find online learning to be a suitable choice.

Additionally, parents or caregivers who might not want to pay to send their child to a private, religiously affiliated school but who still want to incorporate religious aspects into the child's daily routine might find online learning to be the best choice for the student and the family.

Flexibility

Some families are simply looking for more flexibility in their children's learning schedule. Students who have parents whose jobs require the family to travel or students who are training for a specific talent such as ballet or singing may also find it difficult to attend a conventional school.

One of the largest providers of K–12 online learning, K12 Inc., stated that its online school "differs from traditional schools in that classes do not take place in a building, but rather at home, on the road, or wherever an Internet connection can be found" (K12 Inc., 2014b, p. 1).

This flexibility in where and when learning takes place can be important for many families. Rather than having a paid tutor, parents or caregivers who are professional athletes or performers could enroll their child in an online learning environment (K12 Inc., 2014e). This environment might also be beneficial for children of military members (K12 Inc., 2014e). Military personnel move often during their careers and having a child involved in online learning could help to lessen the disruption in learning and transitioning and adjusting to each new school.

The flexibility can also be valuable to students who are practicing for a specialized skill or sport. The time that is required for practice of that skill or sport can be extraordinary and the hours do not always correspond with a conventional school day.

For example, a young student who was training to be a ballerina practiced four times each week and spent as many as eight hours on Fridays honing her craft. She attended an online school and shared her experience in a blog published by CNN:

> Ballet is really important to me and it's usually in the mornings, so if I went to school I would only be able to go on the weekends. Sometimes I'll study in the morning and I'll do a few classes and then I'll go to ballet for maybe like three or four hours and I'll come back home and I'll do some more." (Jones, 2012)

Her story provides a clear example of the flexibility that K–12 online learning can afford.

Highly Qualified Teachers

Not only do proponents of online education in K–12 settings argue that this type of learning provides choice and flexibility for parents, caregivers, and students, they also assert that it can offer access to highly qualified teachers. According to Dan Lips (2010) with the Heritage Foundation, this is particularly important for students who live in areas or attend schools where there is inequitable access to qualified teachers.

In numerous studies, research indicates the importance of teacher quality in student learning outcomes (Betts, Reuben, & Danenberg, 2000; Goldhaber & Brewer, 2000). Unfortunately, there is great disparity in the access that students have to effective instruction and skilled teachers.

For example, Patrick Shields et al. indicated that during the 2001 school year in California, "urban schools, the lowest-performing schools, and schools with high numbers of poor and minority students" bore the brunt of underprepared teachers (2001, p. 22).

By 2014, it seemed not much had improved. In an open letter to colleagues, Catherine Lhamon, the assistant secretary for civil rights, noted that disparities still occurred among districts but they also occurred within districts and even within classrooms housed at the same school (2014). She went on to say the following:

> Schools serving the most black and Latino students are 1.5 times more likely to employ teachers who are newest to the profession (who are on average less effective than their more experienced colleagues) as compared to schools serving the fewest of those students. The unequal provision of strong teachers and stable teacher workforces too often disadvantages the schools with the most at-risk students. (Lhamon, 2014, p. 4)

Some propose that involving students in online learning is one way to solve limited access to experienced teachers. Lips (2014) asserts that online learning can bridge inequities by providing highly qualified teachers to all students, regardless of economics or geography. He goes on to say that K–12 online learning could also help to solve the issue of teacher shortages in high-need areas such as mathematics and science (Lips, 2014). If a student in a traditional school did not have a highly qualified teacher, he or she could learn, online, from a qualified person elsewhere (Lips, 2014).

Cost

Finally, some advocates of online learning propose that this educational format can lower costs while increasing efficiency, thus reducing the strain that is placed on taxpayers (Lips, 2014). Authors of an article in *Forbes* magazine suggested that, due to budget cuts that are taking place in many, if not most, school districts around the nation, the shift or transition to online learning in K–12 settings is not only beneficial but is almost inevitable (Christensen & Horn, 2010).

Christensen and Horn (2010) believe that online learning is a way for educators and taxpayers to do more with fewer funds. For example, they state that those in charge of overseeing schools could save considerable amounts of money if they were to scale back on offering non-core courses in the traditional manner and offer them online.

This would include courses such as foreign language and advanced placement classes. They feel as though this would aggregate demand across numerous school districts and could reduce the number of periods in which classroom courses are held (Christensen & Horn, 2010).

Moe and Chubb (2009) stated that "schools can be operated at lower cost, relying more on technology (which is relatively cheap) and less on labor (which is relatively expensive)" (p. 7). For the schools that are facing budget cuts, Moe and Chubb (2009) believe that they could cut back on approximately one-sixth of their teaching staff if they had students in elementary school spending at least one hour of the day in online learning.

They suggest that these savings could be used to invest in teacher training or to raise teacher salaries, in order to develop highly qualified teachers (Moe & Chubb, 2009). Others disagree and point to the cons of online learning.

Cons

Those who are against or who are skeptical of online learning in grades K–12 provide reasons why they believe this instructional approach to be concerning. As noted in the *New York Times*, the main argument seems to be a lack of evidence to indicate that online learning is superior to traditional, face-to-face instruction (Gabriel, 2011). Due to the lack of research, some feel that online learning is driven by a need or desire to cut costs on resources such as teachers and buildings, rather than a desire to produce a high-quality education (Gabriel, 2011).

There is also the concern that online learning does not equally serve all students (Miron et al., 2013). According to Miron et al. (2013), as compared to traditional schools, virtual schools serve fewer black, Hispanic, poor, and special education students. If online education is to be the "wave of the future," and taxpayer money is being used to fund this type of learning, it is important that all students have equal access.

Evidence

To begin with, the overarching concern regarding online learning seems to be the need for more research regarding its effectiveness. Currently, there is limited evidence, if any, that clearly points to the most conducive approach to learning, whether it be in a traditional face-to-face format or in an online environment (Center for Public Education, 2012; UCLA IDEA, 2013).

In 2009, the U.S. Department of Education conducted a meta-analysis and screened over 1,000 empirical studies, examining online learning in K–12 and postsecondary students (USDE, 2010). After identifying approximately 50 studies that met its criteria of comparing face-to-face and online environments, examining student outcomes with a rigorous research design, and providing enough information to determine an effect size, it found that "on average, students in online learning conditions performed modestly better than those receiving face-to-face instruction" (USDE, 2010, p. ix).

The U.S. Department of Education (2010) also found that there were larger advantages to blended learning, as compared to fully online instruction or fully face-to-face instruction. Additionally, it determined that there was limited research that used a rigorous design and examined the effects of online learning in grades K–12 (USDE, 2010).

As many as 43 studies that were included in the meta-analysis examined the effects of online learning in older learners, leaving questions as to the outcomes for students in grades K–12 (USDE, 2010).

While the meta-analysis is one of the only wide-scale national studies that has been conducted, there is some research that indicates negative effects of online learning in K–12. According to Miron et al. (2013) at the National Education Policy Center, when comparing state ratings, adequate yearly progress (AYP) status, and timely graduation rates, traditional schools outperform virtual schools. However, the authors note that state ratings and AYP status are crude measures for capturing school performance as AYP also includes nonacademic measures such as school attendance (Miron et al., 2013).

Gene Glass and Kevin Welner (2011) also examined research in relation to several facets of online learning, one of which was student achievement. Results indicated that "research in this area is extremely limited. Those making policy should be clear on this key point: there exists no evidence from research that full-time virtual schooling at the K–12 level is an adequate replacement" for traditional learning and/or teaching (p. 5). While it is outside the scope of this chapter to review all literature in the field, clearly, more research is needed on the effects of online learning in K–12 on student achievement.

Serving All Students

Along with a concern about the effectiveness of online learning, there is also the issue of availability and access. In general, it has been argued that virtual schools serve a proportionately lower percentage of students who are economically disadvantaged than do other, traditional public schools (Miron et al., 2013). Based on the national average, it has also been indicated that virtual schools serve almost half the number of students who are classified as being in special education (Miron et al., 2013).

Furthermore, data suggest that fewer black and Hispanic students are enrolled in fully online schools, as compared to the national mean (Miron et al., 2013). Approximately 75% of students in virtual schools are white and of non-Hispanic origin whereas the national average is around 54% (Miron et al., 2013). Providing equal access to all students appears to be a challenge in many areas of the nation.

According to iNACOL (2010), students in online environments must have access to a computer, the Internet, and basic software. While some virtual schools provide those resources, it seems that not all do. This is not a problem for students in affluent areas, but it does pose a problem for those in areas or homes with limited funds or resources (iNACOL, 2010). Additionally, online learning can be challenging for persons with certain disabilities (iNACOL, 2010).

Currently, while equal access remains a challenge, it does appear to be an issue of which online schools are mindful. As the International Association for K–12 Online Learning stated, "Educators must work to ensure that the opportunities of online education are available to students across all income levels, geographic regions, and ethnic groups" (iNACOL, 2010, p. 19).

CONCLUSION

Online learning has gained momentum in the past several years, warranting further investigation into this topic (USDE, 2010, p. xi). In this chapter, terms associated with K–12 online learning were detailed, along with the elements that comprise the online learning framework in grades K–12. Current trends and practices were also discussed and arguments for and against this type of education were presented.

KEY POINTS

- Online learning is a trend that is growing quickly in higher education and in K–12 (iNACOL, 2013b; USDE, 2010).
- It is important to understand terms involved with K–12 online learning. Some terms may seem similar but may have very different meanings.
- It is also important to understand the dimensions and categories that comprise the K–12 online framework. These elements can provide information such as the audience that can be reached, the institutions that are served, whether the learning is full-time or supplemental, and other critical components of online learning in K–12.
- Current trends in K–12 online learning include fully online schools, state virtual schools, course choice programs, distance education programs, and online learning in traditional schools.
- Proponents of online learning in K–12 argue that this type of learning provides choice, flexibility, access to highly qualified teachers, and lower costs. Those against this approach contend that there is not enough research on the effects of online learning on student outcomes and that it is not accessible for all students.

- While the largest study conducted in this field points to the moderate positive effects of online learning in K–12, more research must be conducted.

REFERENCES

Ambient Insight. (2015). *2015 learning technology research taxonomy*. Retrieved from http://www.ambientinsight.com/Resources/Documents/AmbientInsight_Learning_Technology_Taxonomy.pdf.

Babson Survey Research Group. (2015). *K–12 survey reports*. Retrieved from http://www.onlinelearningsurvey.com/k12.html.

Betts, J. R., Rueben, K. S., & Danenberg, A. (2000). *Equal resources, equal outcomes? The distribution of school resources and student achievement in california*. San Francisco, CA: Public Policy Institute of California. Retrieved from ERIC database (ED451291).

Center for Public Education. (2007). *Searching for the reality of virtual schools*. Retrieved from http://www.centerforpubliceducation.org/Main-Menu/Organizing-a-school/Searching-for-the-reality-of-virtual-schools-at-a-glance/Searching-for-the-reality-of-virtual-schools-full-report.pdf.

Center for Public Education. (2012). *Searching for the realities of virtual school at a glance*. Retrieved from http://www.centerforpubliceducation.org/Searching-for-the-reality-of-virtual-schools.

Christensen, C. M., & Horn, M. B. (2010). Education as we know it is finished. *Forbes*. Retrieved from http://www.forbes.com/2010/07/12/education-online-learning-leadership-careers-christensen.html/.

Florida Virtual School. (2014). *Florida virtual school*. Retrieved from http://www.flvs.net/Pages/default.aspx.

Gabriel, T. (2011, April 5). More pupils are learning online, fueling debate on quality. *New York Times*. Retrieved from http://www.nytimes.com/2011/04/06/education/06online.html?=pagewanted=all&_r=1&.

Glass, G. V., & Welner, K. G. (2011). *Online K–12 schooling in the U.S.: Uncertain private ventures in need of public regulation*. Boulder, CO: National Education Policy Center. Retrieved from http://nepc.colorado.edu/publication/online-k-12-schooling.

Goldhaber, D. D., & Brewer, D. J. (2000). Does teacher certification matter? High school teacher certification status and student achievement. *Educational Evaluation and Policy Analysis 23*, 79–86.

Golod, A. (2014, September 19). Online options expanding in higher education landscape. *U.S. News & World Report*. Retrieved from http://www.usnews.com/news/college-of-tomorrow/articles/2014/09/22/online-options-expanding-in-higher-education-landscape.

Horn, M. (2011, May 5). Online learning begins to explode into the mainstream in blended schools [Web log post]. Retrieved from http://www.christenseninstitute.org/online-learning-begins-to-explode-into-the-mainstream-in-blended-schools/.

Huffington Post. (2011, April 13). Online learning: The pros and cons of K–12 computer courses. Retrieved from http://www.huffingtonpost.com/2011/04/12/online-learning-pros-and-cons_n_848362.html.

International Association for K–12 Online Learning (iNACOL). (2010). *A national primer on K–12 learning*. Retrieved from http://www.inacol.org/wp-content/uploads/2012/11/iNCL_NationalPrimerv22010-web1.pdf.

International Association for K–12 Online Learning. (2011). *The online learning definitions project*. Retrieved from http://www.inacol.org/wp-content/uploads/2013/04/iNACOL_DefinitionsProject.pdf.

International Association for K–12 Online Learning (iNACOL). (2013a, February). *Fast facts about online learning*. Retrieved from http://www.inacol.org/cms/wp-content/uploads/2013/04/iNACOL_FastFacts_Feb2013.pdf.

International Association for K–12 Online Learning (iNACOL). (2013b, October). *Fast facts about online learning*. Retrieved from http://www.inacol.org/wp-content/uploads/2013/11/iNACOL-Fast-Facts-About-Online-Learning-October-2013.pdf.

Jones, A. (2012, January 30). Virtual schools on the rise, but are they right for K–12 students? [Web log post]. Retrieved from http://schoolsofthought.blogs.cnn.com/2012/01/30/virtual-schools-on-the-rise-but-are-they-right-for-k-12-students/.

K12 Inc. (2014a). *How a K12 education works*. Retrieved from http://www.k12.com/what-is-k12/how-k12-education-works#.VLb-NHtkZME.

K12 Inc. (2014b). *Online public schools*. Retrieved from http://www.k12.com/schools-programs/online-public-schools#.VP9V6eFkZMG.

K12 Inc. (2014c). *Programs for advanced learners*. Retrieved from http://www.k12.com/who-we-help/advanced-learners-gifted-talented#.VP8xheFkZME.

K12 Inc. (2014d). *Struggling students*. Retrieved from http://www.k12.com/who-we-help/struggling-students#.VP9DSeFkZMF.

K12 Inc. (2014e). *Who we help*. Retrieved from http://www.k12.com/who-we-help#.VMAqZy5kME.

Lhamon, C. E. (2014). Dear colleague letter: Resource comparability. Office of Civil Rights. Retrieved from http://www2.ed.gov/about/offices/list/ocr/letters/colleague-resourcecomp-201410.pdf.

Lips, D. (2010). How online learning is revolutionizing K–12 education and benefiting students. *The Heritage Foundation*. Retrieved from http://www.heritage.org/research/reports/2010/01/how-online-learning-is-revolutionizing-k12-education-and-benefiting-students.

Milpitas Unified School District. (2015). *Blended learning: Beyond using technology*. Retrieved from http://www.musd.org/blended.

Miron, G., Huerta, L., Cuban, L., Horvitz, B., Gulosino, C., Rice, J. K., & Shafer, S. R. (2013). Virtual schools in the U.S. 2013: Politics, performance, policy, and research evidence. In A. Molnar (ed.), *National Education Policy Center*. Retrieved from http://nepc.colorado.edu/files/nepc-virtual-2013.pdf.

Moe, T. M., & Chubb, J. E. (2009). *Liberating learning: Technology, politics, and the future of American education*. San Francisco, CA: Jossey-Bass.

Pearson. (2015). *A better option for hospitalized and homebound students*. Retrieved from http://www.connectionsacademy.com/Libraries/PDFs/CLBP_Homebound.pdf.

Picciano, A. G., & Seaman, J. (2007). *K–12 online learning: A survey of U.S. school district administrators*. Retrieved from http://olc.onlinelearningconsortium.org/publications/survey/K-12_06.

Shields, P. M., Humphrey, D. C., Wechsler, M. E., Riel, L. M., Tiffany-Morales, J., Woodworth, K., Youg, V. M., & Price, T. (2001). *The status of the teaching profession 2001*. Santa Cruz, CA: The Center for the Future of Teaching and Learning.

Staker, H., & Horn, M. B. (2012). Classifying K–12 blended learning. *Christensen Institute*. Retrieved from http://www.christenseninstitute.org/wp-content/uploads/2013/04/Classifying-K-12-blended-learning.pdf.

University of California's Institute for Democracy, Education, and Access. (2013.) *IDEA news: The latest news on what's going on at IDEA*. Retrieved from http://idea.gseis.ucla.edu/newsroom/education-news-roundup/archive/archive-of-education-news-roundup-for-2011/april-2011/online-learning-the-pros-and-cons-of-k-12-computer-courses.

U.S. Department of Education. (2010). *Evaluation of evidence-based practices in online learning: A meta-analysis and review of online learning studies*. Retrieved from https://www2.ed.gov/rschstat/eval/tech/evidence-based-practices/finalreport.pdf.

Watson, J., & Kalmon, S. (2005). *Keeping pace with K–12 online learning: A review of state-level policy and practices*. Retrieved from http://www.learningpt.org/pdfs/tech/Keeping_Pace2.pdf.

Watson, J., Murin, A., Vashaw, L., Gemin, B., & Rapp, C. (2010). *Keeping pace with K–12 online learning: An annual review of policy and practice.* Retrieved from http://www.kpk12.com/wp-content/uploads/KeepingPaceK12_2010.pdf.

Watson, J., Murin, A., Vashaw, L., Gemin, B., & Rapp, C. (2011). *Keeping pace with K–12 online learning: An annual review of policy and practice.* Retrieved from http://www.kpk12.com/wp-content/uploads/KeepingPace2011.pdf.

Watson, J., Murin, A., Vashaw, L., Gemin, B., & Rapp, C. (2013). *Keeping pace with K–12 online and blended learning: An annual review of policy and practice.* Retrieved from http://www.kpk12.com/wp-content/uploads/EEG_KP2013-lr.pdf.

Watson, J., Pape, L., Murin, A., Gemin, B., & Vashaw, L. (2014). *Keeping pace with K–12 digital learning: An annual review of policy and practice.* Retrieved from http://www.kpk12.com/wp-content/uploads/EEG_KP2014-fnl-lr.pdf.

ABOUT THE EDITORS AND CONTRIBUTORS

Stacy Hendricks (Ed.D., Texas A&M University–Commerce) is an assistant professor of educational leadership and coordinator of the Master's in Educational Leadership and Principal Certification Program at Stephen F. Austin State University (SFA), in Nacogdoches, Texas, where she teaches online graduate-level courses to aspiring administrators in the principal preparation program.

Her research interests include online curriculum and pedagogical approaches, educational leadership, and evaluating and improving principal preparation programs. Her research has been published in the *Journal of Online Interactive Learning*, *Online Journal of Distance Learning Administration*, *Education Leadership Review*, *School Leadership Review*, and *Scholar-Practitioner Quarterly*.

After serving 18 years in public education as a teacher and administrator, she transitioned into higher education working as a director of several grants within the SFA James I. Perkins College of Education.

She may be reached at hendricksl@sfasu.edu.

Scott Bailey (Ed.D., Stephen F. Austin State University) is an assistant professor of educational leadership at Stephen F. Austin State University, where he teaches online master's-level courses in the principal preparation program and face-to-face courses on organizational theory and leadership in the doctoral program. Prior to entering academia, he was privileged to serve as a teacher, assistant principal, and principal at the middle and high school levels. He continues to stay connected to public education by working with local districts on school improvement and mentoring beginning teachers, both in association with state agencies. He also trains schools and leadership teams in teacher and principal evaluation.

He may be reached at baileysb73@gmail.com.

* * *

Stephanie B. Applewhite, Ed.D., received her bachelor of behavioral science in social studies in 1995 from Hardin-Simmons University, in Abilene, Texas. She received her master's in secondary education from the University of Phoenix Online in 2004 and her doctorate from Stephen F. Austin State University. Her experiences include working as a social studies teacher, curriculum designer, and high school administrator for 10 years, and she has taught in a variety of environments, including 5–12 private-online, 9–12 charter-public, and as a university instructor. Her research includes online and face-to-face learning experiences, issues of social justice in higher education such as first-generation student success, first-year experiences, high-impact practices, transition, and completion. She has a passion for contributing to rich educational experiences for all students, and uses her organizational, management, teaching, and research background to promote and support engaging educational experiences.

Mary Catherine Breen, Ed.D., is an assistant professor in the Department of Secondary Education and Educational Leadership at Stephen F. Austin State University. She teaches both online and face-to-face graduate and undergraduate educator preparation courses. Dr. Breen has directed two National Professional Development Program grants with the U.S. Department of Education.

Elizabeth Baker Gound, M.Ed., is a 21-year veteran teacher who started her career in public education and is now on her seventh year in higher education. She taught reading for 14 years to students in seventh and eighth grade, serving as UIL coordinator, textbook adoption coordinator, and reading specialist for her academic team. As a member of the Stephen F. Austin State University Secondary Education faculty for seven years, she has created three online courses, teaches both online and face-to-face courses, and works with English language learner programs for preservice teachers. These courses are related to disciplinary literacy, classroom management, diversity, and differentiation. Her research interests include digital literacy, students' successful out-of-school literacy practices, and diversity and struggling readers in public education.

Tracey C. Hasbun, Ph.D., has 14 years' experience as an early childhood and elementary school teacher. She also has eight years' experience in higher education. Currently, she is an assistant professor and NCATE co-coordinator at Stephen F. Austin State University. She serves in the Department of Elementary Education, where she has taught both face-to-face and online courses at the undergraduate and graduate levels. Currently, she teaches online courses in the master's program in early childhood education. These courses include Foundations of Early Childhood, Language and Literacy in Early Childhood, Early Childhood Teaching, Research Analysis Teaching, Intellectual Development of the Young Child, and Psycho-Social Processes of Children. Her research interests include language, literacy, and early childhood studies. She received her doctorate from Texas A&M University, College Station.

Ronny D. Knox, Ed.D., has been in education for the past 25 years. He earned his bachelor's and master's degrees from the University of Houston–Victoria with a focus in educational administration. He received his doctorate in educational leadership from Stephen F. Austin State University. Knox spent the first seven years of his career teaching special education students. He moved into his first principalship in 1998 and has since served as special education director and assistant superintendent of curriculum; he is currently the associate superintendent of business and operations for the Nacogdoches Independent School District in Texas.

Michael Martin, M.Ed., has served in public education for 19 years. He is currently the executive director of human resources for the Nacogdoches Independent School District in Texas. Prior to assuming his current position, he was the director of technology for 10 years and a middle school teacher. He graduated from Texas College with a bachelor's in business administration. He earned his teacher certification, master's in educational leadership, and superintendent certification from Stephen F. Austin State University.

Barbara Qualls, Ph.D., is an assistant professor at Stephen F. Austin State University, teaching in the graduate program for educational leadership. Prior to higher education, she served for over three decades in a spectrum of teaching and leadership positions in Texas public schools, finishing that phase of service as superintendent of a moderately large comprehensive Texas school district. She teaches education law and various courses geared toward the role and skill set of campus leadership. A frequent speaker at professional conferences, she collaborates extensively with the legal and political community in order to keep information and perspectives relevant. Current research activity is centered on the evolution of the governance model, conflict between constitutional civil rights and school safety, and other emerging legal issues. She also serves as treatise chair and advisor for doctoral candidates at Dallas Baptist University.

Pauline M. Sampson, Ph.D., has 27 years' experience in public schools as a teacher, principal, special education director, and superintendent. Additionally, she has 10 years' experience in higher education; she is currently a professor at Stephen F. Austin State University and serves as the superintendent program coordinator and Institutional Review Board chair. She teaches online courses in the superintendent program and courses in the doctoral program. These courses include school finance, facilities and resource management, school law, superintendent seminar, research, paradigms of change, and internship. Her research interests include district leadership of superintendents and school boards, school improvement issues related to science and social studies, and gender studies. She has written five books, three book chapters, two book reviews, and 34 journal articles. Additionally, she has made 76 professional presentations and helped guide 62 doctoral students in their dissertations.

Janet Tareilo, Ed.D., has served in the field of education for the past 33 years. As an educator in the public school system, she has been a classroom teacher, coordinator of a gifted and talented program, and an elementary principal. After receiving her doctorate in educational leadership from Sam Houston State University in 2004, she entered higher education as an assistant professor at Stephen F. Austin State University (SFA) in 2006. In 2010, Dr. Tareilo was awarded the Teaching Excellence Award for the SFA James I. Perkins College of Education. Additionally in 2010, she published a book, *The Other Side of the Desk: A 20/20 Look at the Principalship*, which details her 16 years as an elementary principal. For nine years as an assistant and associate professor in the principal preparation program at SFA, Dr. Tareilo focused on preparing future school leaders. Now, as the associate dean of student services and advising, she works to assist students in completing their college degrees.